ULTIMATE
FOOTBALL

KANTE

FROM THE PLAYGROUND
TO THE PITCH

DINO

First published by Dino Books in 2020,
An imprint of Bonnier Books UK,
The Plaza,
535 Kings Road,
London SW10 0SZ

🔹 @dinobooks
🔹 @footieheroesbks
www.heroesfootball.com
www.bonnierbooks.co.uk

Paperback ISBN: 9781789462302
E-book ISBN: 9781789462319

British Library cataloguing-in-publication data:
A catalogue record for this book is available from the British Library.

Printed and bound in Great Britain by Clays Lltd, Elcograf S.p.A.

1 3 5 7 9 10 8 6 4 2

For all readers, young and old(er)

Matt Oldfield delivers sports writing workshops in schools, and is the author of Unbelievable Football and Johnny Ball: Accidental Football Genius. Tom Oldfield is a freelance sports writer and the author of biographies on Cristiano Ronaldo, Arsène Wenger and Rafael Nadal.

Cover illustration by Dan Leydon.
To learn more about Dan visit danleydon.com
To purchase his artwork visit etsy.com/shop/footynews
Or just follow him on Twitter @danleydon

TABLE OF CONTENTS

ACKNOWLEDGEMENTS

First of all, I'd like to thank Bonnier Books UK – and particularly my editor Laura Pollard – for supporting me throughout and running the ever-expanding UFH ship so smoothly. Writing stories for the next generation of football fans is both an honour and a pleasure.

I wouldn't be doing this if it wasn't for my brother Tom. I owe him so much and I'm very grateful for his belief in me as an author. I feel like Robin setting out on a solo career after a great partnership with Batman. I hope I do him (Tom, not Batman) justice with these new books.

Next up, I want to thank my friends for keeping

me sane during long hours in front of the laptop.
Pang, Will, Mills, Doug, John, Charlie – the laughs
and the cups of coffee are always appreciated.

I've already thanked my brother but I'm also very
grateful to the rest of my family, especially Melissa,
Noah and of course Mum and Dad. To my parents, I
owe my biggest passions: football and books. They're
a real inspiration for everything I do.

Finally, I couldn't have done this without Iona's
encouragement and understanding during long,
work-filled weekends. Much love to you.

CHAPTER 1

WORLD CUP WINNER

15 July 2018, Luzhniki Stadium, Moscow
'N'GOLO KANTÉ!' boomed the tall man with the
microphone, pausing as his words echoed around the
stadium.

N'Golo grinned, looked up at the crowd on
all sides of the pitch and then stepped forward,
through the red, blue and white confetti, to collect
his winner's medal. In a daze, he shook hands with
a long line of FIFA officials. Words came out of
his mouth as he accepted their praise, but later he
couldn't remember any of what he had said to them.

He skipped over to join his teammates, all of
whom had the same smiles all over their faces.

'Congratulations to France, the 2018 World Cup Champions!' Microphone Man screeched.

Fireworks went off all around N'Golo, scaring him for a second, before the music and dancing began. It was party time! After a long month under pressure to bring the trophy home, France had done it. Les Bleus had made up for losing the Euro 2016 Final to Portugal, by winning their second-ever World Cup.

It hadn't always been an easy journey for the team. There had been some nervy moments along the way, like falling 2–1 behind against Lionel Messi's Argentina in the Round of 16, and holding on to beat Eden Hazard's Belgium 1–0 in the semi-final. In the World Cup Final, however, France had cruised to a 4–2 victory over Croatia. It was now official; their talented team was the best in the business.

Allez Les Bleus! Allez Les Bleus!

N'Golo hadn't scored any World Cup goals, but that didn't matter because that wasn't his job. No, France could rely on the skill of Antoine Griezmann, the speed of Kylian Mbappé, and the power of Paul Pogba for that. Instead, N'Golo's job was to do the hard work in midfield, protecting the defence and winning the ball back for the attackers.

And he had played his part brilliantly. His non-stop running had kept Croatia's captain and star player Luka Modrić quiet, just as they had rehearsed in training that week. When N'Golo was substituted in the second half for fresher legs and to avoid picking up a second yellow card, he knew that he had done his job. He and his teammates had saved their best performance for when it mattered the most.

Campeones, Campeones, Olé! Olé! Olé!

As the shiny World Cup trophy was passed from player to player, N'Golo waited patiently for his turn. As usual, he was happy to stay in the background and let others have the spotlight. He liked being the unsung hero.

'Hey, don't forget about N'Golo!' shouted manager Didier Deschamps, spotting that his midfield general was still waiting for his turn.

Finally, the trophy made its way to N'Golo, and his teammates started a little chant of 'Ooooooo!' as he kissed it and lifted it high above his head. He

waved at the three cameras around the stage, hoping
that one of them was the footage that his family
and friends would be watching around the world.
It was a proud, unforgettable night. If people didn't
know the name N'Golo Kanté before the tournament
began, they certainly did now.

As he soaked up the atmosphere, N'Golo had a
strong feeling that this wouldn't be the last time this
team was celebrating a major tournament win. From
the moment the squad arrived in Russia, there had
been a calm confidence amongst the players. And
with Kylian still only nineteen years old, plus Paul,
Antoine and Raphaël Varane all hitting their prime,
the future was incredibly bright for Les Bleus.

'What a night!' Paul yelled in N'Golo's ear as they
waved to the fans and carried the French flag around
the pitch. 'We're World Champions!'

'I like the sound of that,' N'Golo said, grinning
even wider. 'Ever since the '98 World Cup, I've
always dreamed about lifting this trophy, but it's even
more beautiful than it looks on TV.'

'Just wait for the scenes in Paris for the big parade,

my friend! We'll be rock stars for the day.'

'Not bad for two kids who had to do it the hard way,' N'Golo added with a grin.

'That makes it even sweeter,' Paul replied. 'Hopefully some of the youngsters watching tonight will be inspired to follow in our footsteps.'

Kylian suddenly appeared next to them. 'Have you two finished your private meeting yet?' he asked, laughing. 'Come on, we're taking team photos over there!'

N'Golo looked over to the far corner flag. He and Paul had been so distracted that they hadn't even noticed their teammates huddling together for photos. The stadium was still so loud, and none of the France fans wanted to go home.

'Last one there has to sing the anthem on their own!' Paul shouted, sprinting off as N'Golo and Kylian followed.

N'Golo was so serious about his football that it always caught his teammates by surprise in these moments when he let loose, dancing, singing and loving every minute of it. He jumped on Antoine's back and waved his arms from side to side to the beat of the drums in the crowd.

When the celebrations on the pitch finally quietened down, N'Golo and his France teammates got ready for their big team party. Everything had been planned earlier in the week, but it was kept top-secret. No-one had wanted to jinx it.

Sitting in the dressing room, with music blaring in the background and his shin pads scattered across the floor, N'Golo leaned against the wall behind him and closed his eyes for a minute. At twenty-seven years old, he was sure that his football journey still had more twists and turns to come, but it had already been an incredible ride – sometimes painful, sometimes joyful, but rarely dull.

There was no time to dwell on that now, though. Paul appeared out of nowhere, demanding a selfie with him. N'Golo snapped back out of his daydream and grinned for the photo.

CHAPTER 2

FAMILY LIFE IN PARIS

'Kids, let's eat!' Mama called out, turning off the oven and grabbing a stack of plates from the cupboard.

Little N'Golo put his pencil down and rushed to the dinner table. He had learned that it was always better not to make his mum call him a second time.

'What are we having?' he asked as he raced through the kitchen and almost knocked a plate off the counter. 'Sorry!'

Mama gave him a stern look and pointed to his chair. 'If you sit down, you'll find out.'

As Mama laid out the beans and bread, N'Golo licked his lips. There was only enough for a small

portion each, but he never minded that. N'Golo
was still very young, but he already understood the
sacrifices that his parents had made for him and his
brothers and sisters. They worked hard to put food
on the table, but money was always tight. Still, what
the family lacked in fancy things, they made up for
with the constant laughter and music.

They all crowded round the table and tucked
into the food, creating a brief silence before the
conversations started up again. N'Golo took another
piece of bread to mop up the last of his beans while
one of his sisters provided a more detailed recap of
her school dance rehearsal than anyone had asked
for. Still, there was nothing better than being around
the table with the whole family.

After supper, N'Golo put on his pyjamas and lay
down on his bed, waiting patiently for his mum to
come in. Somehow, no matter how tired she was,
she always found time to read a bedtime story to
each of her children.

'Okay, sweetie, do you want me to read you
the rabbit book?' she said eventually, appearing in

the doorway.

N'Golo shook his head. 'Can you tell me the story again of when you moved to France instead?'

His mum smiled. This had become a regular request over the past few weeks. Many years earlier, N'Golo's parents had made the difficult decision to leave their African homeland, Mali, in order to find jobs and a new home in France. There had been ups and downs along the way, but they were proud of the life they had built in Paris.

'Really? You must know that story by heart by now,' she said, sitting down at the end of his bed. 'Aren't you bored of it yet?'

'How could I be?' he said, curling up under his blanket. 'It's our story. I'll never get bored of it.'

When Mama had finished the short version of the story, she smiled at N'Golo. 'And then a few years later, you arrived and gave us even more to be thankful for.'

N'Golo reached across and hugged her. 'You were very brave, Mama. It must have been really scary to move to a totally different country where you didn't know anyone.' He paused, staring at the ceiling. 'I wonder if I'll have adventures like that when I get older. I hope I will.'

His mum fixed his blanket so his legs wouldn't be cold in the night. 'The future holds many amazing things for you, son. I just know it.'

'Hmmm, like what? Will I be an astronaut? Or a racing car driver?'

Mama laughed. 'Those weren't quite the things I had in mind, but you never know. As long as you're happy, I'm happy.'

N'Golo thought about it again. 'No, I don't think I could do things like that. Maybe I can be a footballer instead. My teacher said I'm one of the best in my class and I'm always scoring goals in our playground games.'

'Why not?' his mum replied. She had heard similar things from the rest of the family about how N'Golo came alive when playing football at the park. 'Always dream big, little man,' she said, kissing him on the cheek and turning off the light. 'But even the best football players need their sleep.'

As N'Golo lay there in the dark, he closed his eyes and pictured himself scoring the winning goal in a cup final, with his teammates racing over to hug him and his family cheering in the crowd.

'Why not?' he whispered to himself, repeating his mum's words as he fell asleep.

CHAPTER 3

A FIRST TASTE
OF GLORY

'Come on, we're going to be late!' his dad called
from the doorway. 'If we don't leave now, we'll be
standing for the whole game.'

'But I can't find my blue shirt!' N'Golo replied,
frantically searching all over his bedroom. 'If I don't
wear it and we lose, I'm going to blame myself.'

His dad laughed. 'Typical N'Golo,' he said quietly.

'A-ha, got it!' N'Golo shouted at last. He threw his
other T-shirt onto the bed and pulled on the lucky
blue one. 'Okay, I'm ready to go.'

This particular weekend in July 1998 was different
from every other weekend for one simple reason:
France were in the World Cup Final against the
mighty Brazil. After a lot of phone calls, seven-year-

old N'Golo and his father had found the perfect place to watch the game.

N'Golo was quiet all the way there. His dad watched him in the mirror and guessed what was on his mind. 'Whatever happens, it's an incredible achievement to get this far. Remember, we're the underdogs tonight, so there's less pressure on us to win.'

N'Golo nodded, while looking out of the window. The final was all that N'Golo and his friends had talked about for the last three days. Although he had only seen a few games, he had already decided that Lilian Thuram was his new favourite player.

His dad explained: 'This team has a lot of players whose families have a similar story to ours – leaving Africa or other countries and finding a new home in France. There's Zidane from Algeria, Vieira from Senegal, Thuram from Guadeloupe. It's pretty cool to see them all playing in these big games, isn't it?'

As he watched the players walk out onto the pitch and then sing the national anthems, N'Golo could feel the goosebumps on his arms. These players had the whole country cheering for them. He bit his nails and sipped his water as he waited for kick-off. Even as the fans around him shouted encouragement, he stayed silent. His heart felt like it was beating at double speed.

N'Golo wriggled in his chair as he waited for Emmanuel Petit to swing in the corner, watching as the French players tried to find space in the box. Then it all happened in a blur. He saw Zidane sneak in front of his marker and his header thumped into the net. 1–0! The whole room jumped up at once, hugging and cheering.

Allez Les Bleus! Allez Les Bleus!

As Brazil went looking for an equaliser, N'Golo kept whispering to himself, 'No! No! Clear it! Don't let them score!' He covered his eyes as the French defenders rushed to block a shot. He waved his hand at the screen as if doing that would remind the midfield to track back.

When Zidane made it 2–0 just before half-time, his dad and his brother wrapped N'Golo in a great big hug as total strangers joined them.

'We're really going to do this!' N'Golo shouted to his dad, but it was impossible to hear anything with all the loud cheering. People were standing on tables and one man was even swinging his shirt around his head.

At half-time, N'Golo tapped his fingers on the table as the TV showed the first-half highlights. He was too nervous to even eat the snacks laid out on the table. 'Maybe later,' he said, barely taking his eyes off the screen. The half-time break felt like it would never end.

'Come on, France!'

N'Golo barely moved for the entire second half, apart from biting his nails occasionally. Along with all the other France fans there, he clapped every clearance, cheered every pass and counted down every minute. When Petit scored the third goal in the final seconds, he felt like he could finally breathe again. There was no way that Brazil could stop them now. They were about to become... World Champions!

Outside, they could already hear fireworks going off. N'Golo still had a lot to learn about football, but he understood enough to know that this was the kind of moment that people would always remember – maybe even a once-in-a-lifetime event.

As they began the long walk home, everything was a blur of dancing France shirts and flags. For now, the streets of Paris were painted blue, white and red! Cars blared their horns, music played, and a long night of celebrations was only just beginning. 'That's the power of football,' his dad said. 'No matter what else is going on in life, it can make everything feel better for ninety minutes... or more!'

'Wow, what an amazing feeling that must be, to give the whole country something to cheer about,' N'Golo said, watching the happy scenes in amazement.

What was it his mum had always told him? 'Dream big, little man.'

CHAPTER 4

RUBBISH DUTY

N'Golo put on his shoes as quietly as he could and tiptoed towards the front door. He grabbed his coat from the hook and gently opened the door, looking over his shoulder to check that he hadn't woken anyone up. For the last few weeks, he had started going on early-morning walks to collect rubbish and earn some extra money for the family.

'If you find things that we can recycle, we should be able to pay you a small amount for them,' his boss had explained.

N'Golo loved the challenge. While some of his friends gave up after a few days of work, he walked miles and miles with no complaints. Every week, he tried to cover a few extra streets. It was peaceful when the sun was shining, and he whistled and hummed, miles away in his own little world. Some days were better than others, including one extra special Saturday morning.

'Excuse me,' N'Golo called out to an old man dragging a large rubbish bag to the edge of the pavement, where three other bags were already piled together. 'Can I help you?'

The man looked round, panting heavily, and signalled for him to come over. 'That's a very kind offer, young man,' he said. 'I think I used up all my energy on the first few bags.'

'No problem,' N'Golo replied. He helped to lift the bag and together they placed it next to the others. With the old man's breathing now under control, N'Golo turned to leave and scooped up his own rubbish bag.

'What have you got in there?' the man asked suddenly.

N'Golo hesitated, then decided there was no harm in explaining it. 'It's nothing, really. Just a couple of plastic bottles and other things to recycle. I get a bit of extra money if I come back with some useful stuff – and people throw away some interesting things!'

'Well, let's see if I can help you there,' he replied, reaching for one of the rubbish bags. 'I think I've got some bottles in here.'

The old man dug out two plastic bottles, a milk bottle and some plastic packaging, all of which put a big smile on N'Golo's face.

'Thanks so much!' he said.

'Hang on,' the man added, walking quickly towards his garage, then returning with a big cardboard box. 'I was going to throw this junk out next week too. My grandkids don't play with any of the toys anymore so take anything you want.'

N'Golo's eyes lit up when he looked inside. The toys might have just seemed like junk to the old man, but they were a treasure chest for N'Golo. 'Are you sure you don't want any of these?' he asked, eager to double-check before he got too excited.

The old man nodded and smiled. 'Think of it as a thank you for helping me out.'

N'Golo picked out a few little toy cars for himself and put them in his pocket to take home. Then he filled his bag with all kinds of recyclable things: pieces of a train track, a tea set, a spiral tower and toy fruits.

He skipped back up the street with the bag over his shoulder, turning to wave to the man when he got to the corner.

When he dropped the bag off with his boss, he waited nervously to see his reaction. 'You look pretty pleased with yourself,' his boss said, slumping back in his chair. 'Let's see what we've…'

He paused and raised his eyebrows as he felt how heavy the bag was. Then he took the toys out one by one, and counted the other plastic items. 'Did a school close down or something?' he asked, sounding a little suspicious.

'No, nothing like that. Just a reward for helping someone,' N'Golo replied.

His boss seemed like he wanted to ask more questions, but he just shrugged instead. He reached under the counter and pulled a handful of notes out of his wallet. 'Keep up the great work,' he said, passing the money to N'Golo, whose legs went a bit wobbly at the sight of it.

N'Golo stuffed the money into the pocket of his shorts and rushed home, worrying with every step that he was somehow going to lose it.

'Mama! Mama!' he called as he burst through the door. Even if the money was only enough for a couple of extra things at the supermarket, he was so proud to be helping out.

His mum came charging towards him, with a panicked look on her face. 'What's wrong?'

'Nothing. Sorry, I didn't mean to scare you. It's good news! I found a bag full of stuff this morning on my walk and my boss gave me this.' He reached into his pocket and pulled out the money.

Mama was speechless. She just wrapped N'Golo in a big hug and kissed him on the forehead. 'My son is always full of surprises,' she thought to herself.

CHAPTER 5

JS SURESNES

N'Golo shuffled forward to the front of the line.

'Hi there, are you here for the football trial?' asked a friendly man with a clipboard.

N'Golo nodded and added his name to the list. He had no idea how the trial process worked, but he had heard about the local JS Suresnes team from a friend at school and he wanted to see it for himself. He knew his parents were busy, so he figured out his own way to get to the pitch. The World Cup excitement already seemed like a distant memory, but football had hooked N'Golo. Now he desperately wanted to be part of a team himself, just like Thuram, Zidane and his other France heroes.

The next question totally stumped him. 'So, what position do you play, N'Golo?'

'Well, erm, anywhere except goalie,' he finally replied, shrugging and hoping he didn't sound too silly. He was too small to be a goalkeeper, but he would happily play anywhere else on the pitch.

Clipboard Man passed him a green bib with Number 3 on the back. 'Let's start you as a defender with the green team, then,' he said finally.

Before N'Golo could start walking to the far side of the park, a whistle sounded loudly just behind him. He turned quickly and saw an older, taller man, with a clipboard of his own.

'Good morning, boys!' the man called out. 'For those of you who don't know me, I'm Piotr and I'm the head of the youth teams.'

N'Golo looked around and recognised some of the boys from school. There were a few groups talking and laughing, but he decided to stay where he was so that he could listen to Piotr and work out how to put on the funny-looking bib.

'Thank you all for coming out this afternoon,'

Piotr continued. 'It's nice to see lots of familiar faces from last season and it's exciting to have some newcomers here too. Welcome!'

Out of the corner of his eye, N'Golo watched a couple of the other boys doing some flicks and tricks that he couldn't even dream of pulling off. Still, even if he couldn't match those skills, he was sure he could outrun any of the boys there.

The other boys wearing green bibs called him over. 'Hey, what's your name?'

N'Golo introduced himself and gave a shy wave.

'Cool, I'm Luc,' said a skinny boy with long hair. He pointed to the boy next to him. 'This is Fab.'

'I'm the one who always sets up goals for Luc so he can get all the glory,' Fab said, grinning.

When the six-a-side games started, N'Golo loved the feel of the ball. He was used to old footballs that were on the brink of falling apart. These ones were shiny and new. He cushioned every pass carefully and kept up with even the most skilful players.

'Great tackle!' one of the coaches shouted after N'Golo slid in to stop a promising attack.

Within thirty minutes, N'Golo already felt
like he belonged in the team. He knew what
his main strengths were – tackling, running and
perseverance. He wasn't letting anyone get past him
without a real battle. Luc and Fab were both better
at dribbling and shooting, so N'Golo focused on
getting the ball to them whenever he won it back.

'Thanks, N'Golo!'

The Reds arrived as the next opponent for the
Greens, and N'Golo sprinted to win a tackle within
seconds of the kick-off. He poked the ball to Luc,
who curled a shot just wide.

'Good luck getting the ball past our pitbull,' Fab
called out to the Reds, as N'Golo made another
interception. Soon, the Reds were arguing – 'Keep
it away from Number 3,' one of them shouted
angrily. 'He gets it every time.'

During a quick drink break, Luc patted N'Golo
on the back. 'You're so good!' he said. 'Who did
you play for last year?'

'No-one,' N'Golo said. 'I haven't played for a
team before – just with my brothers at the park.'

Luc almost spilled his drink. 'What?! Never? You can't tell that from the way you play. I'm sure the coaches have already got you on their list for this season.'

'Did you play here last year?' N'Golo asked, suddenly seeing a chance to learn more about the team as well as making a new friend.

Luc nodded. 'And I'm never leaving – playing for JS Suresnes is the best! They make everything fun and it's not just about winning. The coaches really want us to play good football.'

'Are there a lot of spaces left in the squad?'

'At least three or four, I think. A couple of players have left and one of our midfielders is injured for the whole season.'

N'Golo had plenty more questions to ask, but they would have to wait until after the last game of the session. The Yellows were passing the ball around on the pitch behind them, and they looked confident about winning.

'Let's go,' Luc said, high-fiving N'Golo. 'We can't let these boys end our unbeaten run!'

Five minutes later, the Greens were 3–0 up and more of the coaches had gathered on the touchline. 'Good to see you've finally come to watch the best team!' Fab cheekily called over to Piotr with a big grin on his face.

Piotr laughed, but his attention had already been drawn to the little Number 3 who always seemed to be in the right place to win the ball back. He was easily the smallest player on the pitch, but he worked twice as hard as anyone else.

'We've been playing for almost two hours,' Piotr said to Jean, one of the other coaches. 'But Number 3 looks like he could play for two more!'

'Looks like we might have found the midfield engine we were searching for,' Jean replied.

'What's his name?' Piotr asked.

'N'Golo Kanté,' Jean replied, glancing down the list of names.

'Well, let's make sure we talk to him before he leaves. We need to get him signed up before another team beats us to it.'

CHAPTER 6

STAYING STRONG

'Campeones, Campeones, Olé, Olé, Olé!'

N'Golo sang along with his team-mates as they passed the youth cup trophy around. It was the perfect way for him to end his dream debut season at JS Suresnes. And their magnificent midfield dynamo was already looking forward to lifting a few more next year...

But just days after the joy of winning the cup and being named Player of the Tournament, N'Golo's world was turned upside down.

Mama gathered the children around the table and, in a quiet, gentle voice, explained that their father had died that afternoon. N'Golo tried to keep listening but his head was already spinning. They sat and talked for hours – there were tears, hugs, more tears and more hugs.

As he lay in bed, N'Golo wondered what this would mean for the family. Would they have to move back to Mali? Would they have enough money to survive? Eventually, his eyelids got heavy. But before he fell asleep for the night, he made a promise to himself that he would make his father proud – at home, at school, and on the football pitch.

Even though very few people at JS Suresnes had met N'Golo's parents, word spread quickly. His teammates rallied together to try to cheer him up, and Piotr called him into his office at the end of the training session.

'N'Golo, I was so sad to hear the news. How are you doing?'

He shrugged. 'Okay, I guess. It still doesn't feel real.'

'Well, take as much time as you need. If it helps to miss a few games to spend more time with your family, you have our full support. I'm sure there's a lot on your mind at the moment.'

'Actually, football helps, and I think my dad would have wanted me to keep on playing.'

Piotr nodded. 'I can understand that. But the offer is always there if you change your mind.'

The next few months were difficult. N'Golo did more jobs around the flat – washing up, laundry, cleaning – while Mama took on extra hours at work. The Kantés were already living on a very small budget, but now every euro was even more precious.

Despite all the uncertainty at home, N'Golo was as good as ever on the pitch. Piotr watched in admiration as his star midfielder blocked everything else out and ran tirelessly for ninety minutes every week. Although he rarely wanted the praise or attention, he had become the most complete player on the team.

N'Golo had always been quietly competitive, but he was slowly finding his voice too. On a cold, windy morning against their local rivals, JS Suresnes gave away two goals in the first ten minutes. N'Golo saw his teammates' heads dropping all around him.

They were second to every loose ball and they were making mistake after mistake. By half-time, it was 3–0 and the changing room was quiet. He saw Luc and others staring down at the ground.

For the first time ever, N'Golo stood up and shouted. He had plenty to say: 'What's going on? We're acting like we've already lost! There's still forty-five minutes to go. So far, they want this game more than us. Let's change that. Win every tackle, chase every ball. If we get one goal back early, we'll get them rattled. Come on!'

Once the shock of seeing N'Golo speaking up like that wore off, his teammates joined in.

'Yeah, let's go, boys!'

'We're better than these guys!'

The second half was one that Piotr would never forget. From the kick-off, N'Golo thundered into two tackles, winning the ball cleanly and leaving a trail of bodies on the ground. He chased a long ball from Luc and hurried the full back into knocking it out for a corner. Fab swung the ball in and Luc powered a header into the top corner. 3–1!

'Get in!' he screamed. 'We're back in it.'

It was non-stop pressure from that point onwards.
N'Golo covered every blade of grass, intercepting
passes and snatching the ball from every heavy
touch. From one bad clearance, he pounced on the
ball in midfield and sprinted forward. He wanted
to get the ball to one of the strikers but, seeing that
both were tightly marked, he just kept running. He
kicked the ball past the last defender and raced clear.
Before the defender could recover, N'Golo fired the
ball across the box and Fab tapped it in at the back
post. 3–2!

N'Golo clapped every good pass and urged his
teammates to keep running. 'Another goal is coming,
guys!' he shouted. He jumped highest to win a
header in midfield, sending the ball looping forward.
Two defenders hesitated and Luc burst through. He
took the ball round the goalkeeper and calmly slotted
it into the net. 3–3!

On the touchline, the JS Suresnes substitutes and
coaches were high-fiving and cheering. There were
still fifteen minutes to go – could they really go on

and win this?

Their rivals were exhausted. N'Golo could see it in their faces. 'They thought the game was over at half-time,' he said to himself with a little determined smile.

The muscles in his legs were sore, but he refused to slow down. N'Golo thought about what his dad would have thought about a game like this, and that gave him an extra jolt of energy. As the JS Suresnes players pushed forward for a winning goal, their rivals won the ball back. Three quick passes later, they had three attackers against two JS Suresnes defenders.

N'Golo spotted the danger and sprinted towards it as fast as he could. He could see where the final pass was going to go, and he threw himself in the way at full stretch, getting the tiniest touch to knock the ball away for a corner. As he got up, five of his teammates rushed to hug him.

'How did you get to that?!' Luc asked in amazement.

Pierre, the goalkeeper, ruffled his hair. 'You really

saved us there!'

Two minutes later, N'Golo was on another big run – this time towards the opposition goal. He played a quick one-two on the right wing and, as he reached the return pass, he knew his legs wouldn't allow him to dribble further. He had to cross it in now.

N'Golo kicked the ball as firmly as he could but he mishit it in a moment of panic. It spun wildly – much closer to the goal than he had intended. He watched as the ball dipped, almost in slow motion, over the hands of the goalkeeper who was back-pedalling desperately. Was it going in? N'Golo's heart sank as the ball bounced off the crossbar, but he was jumping in the air seconds later as Fab bundled in the rebound. 4–3 to JS Suresnes!

Their incredible comeback was complete! N'Golo threw himself on the ground. He was too tired to even run over to celebrate with his teammates. Instead, Luc, Fab and the others raced over to him, diving on top of him in one giant pile. Their rivals barely had time to kick off before the referee blew the final whistle. N'Golo put both arms in the air as they all hugged again.

'What a game! What a win!' N'Golo shouted, as they all struggled to catch their breath.

The coaches were still in disbelief as they tried to deliver a post-game team talk.

'There's nothing left to say after a second half like that,' one of the coaches said. 'N'Golo, I think we better let you give the team talks from now on!'

CHAPTER 7

NOTHING LEFT TO CHANCE

The next year was a similar story, with N'Golo pushing his JS Suresnes team to new heights.

'You may not get as much attention as the boys who score the goals, but this team wouldn't be the same without you controlling the midfield,' Piotr said proudly, putting an arm round N'Golo as they walked side-by-side towards the changing room after the last game of the season.

'Thanks, coach,' N'Golo said. It was always nice to hear that kind of praise, but at the same time he never knew what else to say. He was just happy that the team was winning.

'Enjoy your summer break, but don't let yourself

get too comfortable.'

N'Golo turned to his coach with a confused look on his face. 'What do you mean?'

Piotr paused, then added, 'You're a special player. Every manager in the league wishes that you were playing for them. But there are always ways to get better. During the summer, think about what you can improve on to become an even more complete midfielder.'

'I could grow a bit, I guess!' N'Golo teased.

'Well, I was thinking of something a bit easier to control!' Piotr replied. 'The one thing that I noticed this season is how much you use your right foot for everything – passing, shooting, dribbling. The game will feel even easier for you if you're confident enough to use your left foot as well. Start with simple passes and go from there.'

N'Golo nodded. It was a good point. He always liked to get the ball onto his right foot, especially if he was under pressure. 'This is my one summer project,' he announced that night at supper.

'Your second summer project, you mean,'

Mama corrected him. 'Don't forget about all your schoolwork that has to be done!'

'Oh yes, right,' N'Golo replied quickly. But he had already begun planning how he could work on his left foot. After supper, he pulled out an orange cone that he had kept from one of his early morning recycling hunts. He had used it many times as one of the goalposts at the park. Now, it was going to come in handy to practise passing with his left foot. N'Golo brushed the dust off the cone and put it in his school bag, along with a mini football that he had been given by Piotr.

On his way home from school the next day, he took a different route, stopping at a park that he knew would be quiet. N'Golo placed the cone on the grass and walked back twenty steps, counting out loud. He put the ball down at his left foot and lined up the pass, aiming for the middle of the cone.

His first attempt was too slow and trickled to a stop before it even reached the cone. N'Golo looked around, hoping no one else had seen that. His second attempt skidded past, only just missing the cone.

His third try smashed into the middle of the cone, knocking it over.

'Yes!' he shouted.

Some boys might have been satisfied with hitting the cone two or three times out of ten, but N'Golo was aiming higher. 'If I want to be a professional footballer, I need to be good with both feet,' he had told his friends that morning. 'Trust me – by the end of the summer, you won't be able to tell which is my weaker foot!'

They all laughed – not because they didn't believe him, but because they knew that N'Golo was determined enough to actually do it.

As it got darker and darker at the park, N'Golo continued his quest for the perfect ten out of ten. He got eight, then eight again, then nine, yelling in frustration as he dragged the tenth pass just wide of the cone. Finally, he nailed all ten, sprinting across the grass as if he had scored the winning goal in a cup final. Even after one afternoon of practice, he felt a little more comfortable using his left foot.

When preseason rolled around, Piotr grinned

as he watched 'The New N'Golo' on the ball. He could immediately see that his little midfielder had worked hard during the summer. At the end of the first training session, the ball dropped to N'Golo just outside the penalty area. Without even thinking about it, he swung his left foot at it and watched as the shot rocketed into the bottom corner.

Goooooooooooooooooooaaaaaaaaaaaaaaaaallllllllllll lllllllllllllll!!!!!!!!!!!!!!!!!!!!!

N'Golo turned to Piotr on the touchline and winked.

'That kind of dedication is really rare,' Piotr said to the other coaches as they huddled later that afternoon. 'I made one suggestion, and he spent a whole summer proving me wrong.'

That was just one of many ways in which Piotr challenged N'Golo to keep adding to his game. After one loss where the whole team was overpowered by bigger, stronger opponents, he saw another opportunity to nudge N'Golo forward.

'That was a tough one tonight. We had more talent than them, but they were first to everything.'

N'Golo nodded, staring at the ground.

'But you're going to come up against a lot of midfielders like that. You're strong enough to stand up to it, but we need to work on your heading. Even at your height, you've got the spring in your legs to challenge for high balls.'

Just like that, Piotr had put a new project in N'Golo's head – and, once again, he had a creative solution for practising. But he was going to need some help.

After much persuasion and the promise of taking over some of his household chores, one of his brothers agreed to be the ballboy. That involved not only collecting the ball each time but also throwing it up high for N'Golo to jump up and head away. At first, it was a slow process and N'Golo couldn't always control where the ball ended up. But soon he was timing his jumps better and heading the ball with confidence. Even when his legs ached, he jumped again and again.

'Thanks, these are the things I have to get right if I want scouts to pay attention,' he told his brother as they walked home. 'Most of them are going to think I'm too small, but I just need one scout to believe in me – that's all.'

'Well, I was sweating just watching you do all that heading,' his brother replied, laughing. 'You're a natural. So you can tell those scouts to come and talk to me if they don't think you're big enough to make it!'

CHAPTER 8

DOMINATING LIKE DIARRA

Back when N'Golo first joined JS Suresnes, he had struggled with the question of which position he should play. Within a few games, however, the right answer had become clear – central midfielder. The role suited his high-energy style and it also allowed him to follow in the footsteps of one of his latest football heroes, Lassana Diarra.

He had first seen Diarra on TV at a friend's birthday party. That day, the boys gathered in the lounge to watch a French league game, and Diarra turned out to be the star player. Officially, he played in defensive midfield for Le Havre, but really, he was everywhere, racing all over the pitch.

'He reminds me of you,' the birthday boy said, poking N'Golo in the ribs. 'He never stops moving!'

N'Golo smiled. He was thinking the same thing. 'Well, maybe there's a chance for me after all,' he replied. 'He's pretty small too!'

As he said it, Diarra slid in to win another tackle and laid the ball off to a teammate. A few of his friends went off to play video games, but N'Golo stayed in his chair, glued to the game.

For the next few months of playground games, while his friends pretended to be the world's biggest stars – like Thierry Henry and Zidane – N'Golo always played as his new hero.

'Diarra wins another loose ball,' he called out, intercepting a pass and providing commentary at the same time. 'He sprints forward and plays the ball through... and, oh, just wide.'

'I want to be Diarra today,' one of his friends shouted later that week as they set up the goalposts.

'Me too,' added another.

'Don't even think about it!' N'Golo snapped, tying his shoelace. 'You don't even like him. I've told you before...'

As he turned around, he saw they were all
giggling. He had fallen for it. 'Good one!' he said,
smiling. 'But deep down, I know that you all wish
you could be Diarra.'

When N'Golo's birthday arrived, Mama put his
presents on the table along with a small cake. She
wanted everything to be just right.

In the middle of the table was a big envelope that
she had found under the door earlier in the week
when she got home from work. N'Golo's name was
scribbled on the front, but she had no idea who it
was from.

N'Golo woke up and stumbled into the kitchen,
still half asleep. 'HAPPY BIRTHDAY!' his family
all shouted, making him jump. He put on his
birthday hat and eyed the chocolate cake. It was his
favourite. Then he picked up the big envelope and
looked at the handwriting on the front. It didn't look
like anyone's in his family. Hmmm, so who could it
be from?

He decided to open that envelope first. He ripped

off the flap, reached inside and felt a sheet of paper. He glanced around the table, but no one seemed to know what it was.

N'Golo pulled the paper out and saw it was a folded, glossy poster. When he unfolded it, he jumped out of his chair. 'Oh, wow!' he shouted. 'Diarra – I've got to put this up on the wall!' He disappeared to his bedroom to find the perfect spot.

The rest of the family followed, watching from the doorway as N'Golo unpinned a school certificate from just above his bed and put up his Diarra poster instead.

'Who is it from?' he asked suddenly. 'There wasn't a note or card inside the envelope.'

'We don't know,' Mama explained. 'It just appeared one afternoon. But I think almost everyone around here knows that Diarra is your favourite player, so good luck figuring it out! It could be any of our neighbours, or someone from your school, I guess.'

Year after year, the poster stayed up on the wall as N'Golo continued to watch as many of Diarra's games as possible, trying to copy the way that he passed, dribbled and tackled. All of that came in handy as the JS Suresnes coaches pushed him to the limit, promoting him to the older age groups to play against boys three or four years older than him.

'Don't worry,' he reassured Mama when he saw concern in her eyes. 'I can handle it, just like Diarra does. He's small too.'

'But you're half their size!' she groaned. 'I don't understand. What's the rush?'

'They want to help me get better faster. I'm doing really well in the Under 15s, but playing with the Under 18s will teach me so much more. I might not start every game, but I'll be able to learn lots from the older boys.'

Mama still wasn't sure, but she trusted N'Golo to make the right decision. 'If you start coming home with all kinds of injuries then this has to stop, okay?' she said, wagging her finger.

'OK, but I'll be fine,' N'Golo said, grinning. 'If things get too tough, I'll just run through their legs!'

CHAPTER 9

FAN FAVOURITE

'There he is!' N'Golo heard one fan shout, pointing in his direction. 'Give us a wave!'

'I love that kid,' added the man next to him. 'I just hope he doesn't leave us.'

It was still just the warm-up at JS Suresnes' third game of the season but, as usual, there were lots of fans already crowded around the pitch – all eager to see N'Golo play.

'You're a local celebrity now,' his teammate Richard joked, playfully shoving N'Golo. 'I could score the goal of the season and they'd still be hugging you at the end of the game.'

'Not this again!' N'Golo said, rolling his eyes, then

grinning. 'I'll give you my autograph if that's what this is really about.'

It was a strange feeling for N'Golo. In many ways, he was hoping that a bigger team would swoop in to sign him, but he also enjoyed being close to home and playing with friends that he had known for years.

N'Golo's rise at JS Suresnes had become legendary. He was still just sixteen years old but had become a key part of the Under 18s team, despite being the smallest player on the pitch in most games. He was happy to be the little underdog who the opposition didn't take seriously enough until it was too late.

Today was no different. In the first few minutes of the game, after N'Golo won a header, he heard a defender shout to a tall beanpole teammate: 'You should be winning every ball in midfield. Look at the size of him!'

'Easy pickings,' Beanpole replied, giggling.

N'Golo smiled to himself. 'Uh oh,' whispered Frederic, another midfielder, as he jogged past. 'I guess they don't know that it's never wise to get you fired up like that!'

For the next eighty minutes, N'Golo made life really miserable for Beanpole. Each time he cut out one of his passes or took the ball away after a loose touch, he could sense that Beanpole was getting angrier and angrier. 'Argh, come on!' he yelled as N'Golo nipped in front of him and cleared the ball out for a throw-in.

Not content with just ruining Beanpole's day, N'Golo also set up the winning goal too. When the ball looped up in midfield, he got there first and controlled it on his chest. After a quick look up to see what his options were, he dribbled forward and slid a perfect pass through for Rami, the team's top scorer. Rami held off his defender, knocked the ball round the keeper and tapped it in. He slid on his knees over near the touchline, then turned to point at N'Golo.

'What a pass!' he called out.

At the final whistle, N'Golo took off his shin pads and high-fived Frederic. Beanpole appeared next to him and offered a handshake. 'You were awesome today. I feel kind of silly for thinking that it was going to be an easy game just because you're a lot smaller. You sure showed me!'

N'Golo shrugged and smiled. 'Thanks. You're not the first to think that – and I bet you won't be the last either!'

As they walked off the pitch together, the quiet crowd suddenly got loud again as fans rushed forward to cheer N'Golo off the pitch.

'Great game, little man!' called one woman, wearing a scarf in the team colours – yellow and blue.

'Kanté! Kanté! Kanté!' chanted a group of teenagers, who all looked older than him.

Back in the changing room, the JS Suresnes players turned up the volume on the sound system and swapped stories about the game.

'Great win, lads. I thought you were going to miss that one, Rami!'

'So did I, mate, with that giant centre-back breathing down my neck!'

'N'Golo, what were you chatting about with that beanpole after the game? Did you say sorry for embarrassing him like that all game long?'

N'Golo smiled and shrugged. He wasn't a big, loud character like some of his teammates. Out on the football field, he just got on with his job – winning the midfield battle. As he began walking away from the stadium, Frederic called out from across the car park. 'Well played today, mate. Do you need a lift to the bus stop?'

'That would be amazing. Thank you, my legs could do with a break!'

Frederic swung the car round and N'Golo hopped in.

'Those guys were pretty cocky at the start today,' Frederic said, smiling. 'By the second half, they didn't have much to say, though.'

N'Golo laughed. 'Yeah, I think that was one of our best games of the season. There's nothing better than proving people wrong.'

When Frederic dropped him off and turned to rejoin the traffic, he shook his head. 'In many ways, he's still just a shy kid,' he said to himself. 'But then on the pitch, he turns into an unstoppable bulldog.'

CHAPTER 10

WAITING...
AND WAITING

As much as N'Golo enjoyed winning games with JS Suresnes, he was starting to think about taking on a new challenge. Through the youth team years, he had always been battling to keep up with older boys. Now, things felt a bit too comfortable.

But that next step was proving harder than he had expected.

'You can add these to the pile,' N'Golo said one morning, walking into the kitchen and throwing two letters down on the counter angrily. 'Rennes and Lorient have also both said no to a trial.'

He stormed up to his room and sat on the edge of his bed, with tears trickling down his cheeks. 'It's not fair,' he said to himself. 'What else can I do?'

Mama gave N'Golo a few minutes to calm down. She knew how good he was at finding his way back to the positives. Sure enough, he soon reappeared in the kitchen. She hugged him tightly.

'Be patient, sweetie. The right team is out there somewhere. They just haven't found you yet.'

'But people are always telling me that the chances of making it as a professional footballer are tiny. How can you be so sure?'

'Because I know you, and I believe in you,' she said.

'I just wish teams focused on what I can do, instead of what they think I can't do.'

N'Golo's main problem was still his height. The top teams just weren't interested in little guys like him, even though he was brave enough to out-battle all the big boys he played against. Sadly, they only wanted tall, powerful players.

It was hard to sit there and wait. Two other JS Suresnes players had just moved to Ligue 2 teams after catching the eye of the visiting scouts, but apparently no-one was asking about N'Golo, even when he approached them directly for a trial.

'But what if no-one gives me a chance?' he asked Mama later that same week as the doubts came flooding back again. 'I know I'm good enough to play at a higher level, and I'm at least as good as the boys who are getting contracts. I just don't understand why the scouts can't see that!'

'N'Golo, all you can do is use it as extra motivation to keep getting better. Make it impossible for the scouts to ignore you. If they have a certain type of player in mind, make them rethink that by bringing another option to the table.'

He kept those words in mind for the rest of the season. When most players were starting to tire in the second half of games, N'Golo clenched his fists and kept running. He got stuck into even more tackles and battled even harder for every header. No-one was going to push him around.

When they played the team at the top of the table, N'Golo was the best player on the pitch. But even when JS Suresnes won 3–1, he just walked over to pick up his water bottle. No big deal! He was only doing his job.

'Most of the best athletes in the world got to the top of their sport partly because of the way they used every snub as extra motivation,' Piotr explained when he saw the sad look on N'Golo's face. 'Keep your head up and keep going!'

The other coaches were unsure what to say – he was their standout player, but he seemed so distant and downhearted. It was as if the rejections from other clubs were really weighing on his mind.

N'Golo played with an edge all year and the team brushed aside not only their league opponents but also some of the best teams in the regional cup competition. He was doing everything he could to catch the eye of any scouts on the touchline.

'I want to help him find a bigger club just so we don't have to play against him anymore,' one manager said to Piotr at an end-of-season awards dinner. He was only half-joking.

CHAPTER 11

A BIG BREAKTHROUGH AT BOULOGNE

N'Golo was still hopeful about his football career, but he was nineteen years old now and it was time to start thinking about other options in case a promising door didn't open. Then he got the call that changed everything.

He was reading a book in his room on a Thursday night when he heard the phone ring. Mama answered. After a few seconds of quiet, she shouted out, 'N'Golo, it's for you!'

He walked quickly to the kitchen, assuming it was one of his friends from school asking about a homework project or his plans for the weekend.

'Who is it?' he whispered to his mum.

'Piotr. He says it's important.'

N'Golo froze. Piotr rarely called him at the house. He picked up the phone. 'Hi!'

'Hi, N'Golo. Sorry to bother you but this couldn't wait until Saturday. Jean-Pierre has been talking with Boulogne and they want to sign you.'

'Jean-Pierre' was Jean-Pierre Perrinelle, the JS Suresnes Club President.

As the amazing news sunk in, N'Golo put his hand on the kitchen counter to steady himself. 'Wow!' was all he could say.

'I know! This could be the big break you've been waiting for. They aren't promising anything long-term, but they want to give you a shot.'

'That's amazing! So, well, how... what... how does it work? Do I just show up there?'

'Don't worry, one of their coaches is going to send me all the details,' Piotr explained. 'If you're still planning to drop by on Saturday, I'll give you an update. Then I'm sure they'll be in touch directly after that.'

By now, Mama and his brothers had heard

the excitement in N'Golo's voice, and they were standing in the doorway, straining to hear the conversation. 'So?' they said in chorus once he had put the phone down.

'I'm going to be signing for Boulogne!'

They rushed over and hugged him tightly. 'I'm so happy for you,' Mama said, a tear rolling down her cheek next to a big smile. 'But we're really going to miss you!'

Boulogne, based in Boulogne-sur-Mer, was almost three hours away, so N'Golo had no choice but to move. His contact at Boulogne helped book his travel and arranged a room for him, close to the club's stadium.

The idea of leaving the flat and moving away from his family and friends was scary, but at the same time, N'Golo felt so excited about following his professional football dream. If his parents could move all the way from Mali to France, then he was sure that he could handle a few miles. Still, it was a hard thing to talk about. As he packed his bag, he aimed to bring only the true essentials – but the pile kept getting bigger and bigger.

'How are you going to get to training?' his brother asked as they talked about his new routine. 'You'll probably have to take your driving test.'

N'Golo already had a plan for that. 'I'll be able to walk to the stadium for games,' he explained. 'Plus, I've got my micro scooter for getting to training.'

His brother started laughing, but then realised that N'Golo was being serious. 'Oh, right. Are you sure you want your new teammates to see you arrive on a micro scooter?'

N'Golo shrugged. He never really cared what other people thought. 'Well, I'm sure they'll be a bit jealous, but that's okay!' he said with a great big grin.

'Somehow, I doubt that will be their first reaction, smart guy,' his brother said, giving him a playful punch.

But once N'Golo got to his new home, he immediately saw that the scooter might not have been the best choice. Boulogne was full of hills and uneven ground. He hated being late for anything, so he left the flat even earlier than necessary to allow for extra time. Going uphill, he felt the scooter might fall apart at any moment as it creaked and wobbled.

Away from home, N'Golo also found that he suddenly had a lot more free time, without his close group of friends to meet up with, or family to see regularly.

'Why don't you find a course or a class to go to?' Mama suggested on the phone one night. 'I remember there were some classes that you wanted to sign up for a few years ago but at the time you couldn't because of your football.'

N'Golo thought about that over the next week and picked up some leaflets from the local colleges and universities. In the end, he settled on a diploma in accountancy. He had always enjoyed working with numbers.

But his Boulogne teammates had other ideas for how he could spend some of his spare time. 'There are so many parties around town, and we can easily get you in,' one of the older players explained.

'There's a new place that just opened,' another said. 'We're all going on Sunday night. Come on, Professor, you've got to join us this time.'

N'Golo's answer was always the same, though. 'Sorry, lads, but that's not my scene. Have fun and I'll see you all at training.'

Though N'Golo's teammates were always disappointed and wished they could get to know him better, they at least respected how firmly he stuck to his decisions. Plus, if it meant he kept up his quality performances on the pitch, they would settle for that.

After spending his first season at Boulogne in the reserves, N'Golo had worried about his future at the club, especially after they were relegated down to Ligue 3. But those fears didn't last very long because he was moved up to the first team squad for the start of the 2012/13 season.

As he warmed up with his teammates before an August clash with Luzenac, he took a deep breath to calm himself. 'You're here because you're good enough,' he told himself. A few of the older players gave him a pat on the shoulder, sensing his nerves.

'Just relax, kid – you'll be great!'

Once the game started, N'Golo snapped into a different level of focus. The pre-practice nerves disappeared completely as he raced around the midfield, protecting the space in front of the defenders and playing quick, short passes to start the counter attacks.

'Great pass, N'Golo,' shouted Georges Tournay, the Boulogne boss, who had spent part of his team talk urging his players to always look for the simple pass and keep the ball on the ground.

When one of the Luzenac players received treatment for an injury, Georges called N'Golo over to the touchline. 'If you see we've got plenty of cover at the back, don't be shy about pushing forward a bit. We're getting good crosses into the box, but there's no-one on the end of them.'

N'Golo nodded. He knew his first job was always to do the tough defensive work, but that didn't stop him from working on his shooting in training.

Ten minutes later, Alexis Allart, the team's star

man, started a dribbling run on the right wing. N'Golo looked over his shoulder and, spotting that there were three Boulogne defenders marking one striker, he sprinted forward. Alexis cut back onto his left foot and scuffed a cross into the box. As two defenders made a mess of their clearances, the ball rolled free towards N'Golo.

What an opportunity! He didn't even hesitate, poking a low shot into the bottom corner.

Goooooooooooooooooooaaaaaaaaaaaaaaaaalllllllllll llllllllllllllllll!!!!!!!!!!!!!!!!!!

N'Golo froze. What was he meant to do? It had been years since he had worked on a goal celebration. He just ran over to the corner flag with one arm in the air as his teammates wrapped him in hugs.

'Nice finish, little man,' Alexis said, putting his arm around N'Golo. 'You even made my terrible cross look good!'

N'Golo was quickly back into his usual role, popping up all over the pitch to win tackles and stop the Luzenac strikers.

'Argh!' one of them yelled, tripping N'Golo in frustration after losing the ball. It was just so annoying to play against someone who seemed to be in so many different places at once!

There was nothing better than a solid 1–0 win in N'Golo's mind, especially when he had scored the winning goal. As he walked off the pitch and clapped to the home fans, Alexis appeared next to him, holding the match ball.

'Here you go, hotshot,' he said, passing the ball to N'Golo. 'You earned it.'

That night, N'Golo spent what felt like hours on the phone with Mama and the rest of the family. They all wanted to get the play-by-play account of his goal.

'We knew there was a superstar striker hidden away there somewhere!' they joked.

N'Golo laughed along, still clutching the match ball under his arm. All of his teammates had signed it after the game, and he was excited to find the right spot for it in his new bedroom.

Whether it was because of his ability to say no to

the night life, or the balance provided by his college class, or just his hunger to take the next step in his career, N'Golo was now thriving at Boulogne. However, he was quickly outgrowing life in Ligue 3.

All of the coaches could see that he was destined for a bigger stage, and so it was no great surprise when other clubs started calling with offers for Boulogne's star midfielder. N'Golo heard a few whispers about a possible transfer but there was no official news yet.

'Let's just wait and see what happens next,' he told himself, not wanting to get too carried away.

Over the summer, N'Golo went back to Paris and caught up on all the latest news. He needed a break from football, but most of all, he needed some of Mama's home cooking.

While he was there, he finally got the call that confirmed he was on the move again – and heading in the right direction. Caen, one of the rising teams in Ligue 2, had clinched a deal to add N'Golo to their midfield.

Mama screamed when she heard the good news.

'This is just the next step!' she told her son with total confidence. 'Once word really spreads, all the top teams will be knocking on the door.'

CHAPTER 12

LEADING CAEN TO LIGUE 1

N'Golo sensed a special mood and togetherness within the Caen squad from the very start of preseason training, especially when the drills and mini games started.

'We have a chance to do something special this season,' said Franck Dumas, one of the co-managers. 'We'll play it cool with the media, of course, but I want us to have really high expectations as a group. Look around you – this is a very talented bunch of players. Promotion is a realistic aim this year, so let's achieve it!'

N'Golo smiled. It was refreshing to hear such a bold statement.

Franck tapped him on the shoulder at the end of
the first meeting. 'We'll be counting on you to run
the show in midfield this season. That's going to be
the key to beating some of these teams with bigger
budgets and deeper squads. We all think you're
ready for it.'

N'Golo tried to keep a serious face and hide a
little smile. 'I'll do everything I can, boss,' he said.

It didn't take long for him to live up to that
promise. On his debut, N'Golo dominated the game
and he carried that confidence into the next game
against Laval too. A new season was always special,
and he got the usual goosebumps as he lined up
with his teammates. He could hear the crowd
roaring as the referee led the teams onto the pitch.

N'Golo never liked to concede goals, but the
challenge of fighting back often took his play to
another level. When Laval scored first, he shook
his head and clapped his hands. 'Let's go,' he
whispered to himself.

His teammates watched in amazement as N'Golo
crunched his way into tackle after tackle, and won

headers against players who were ten years older and six inches taller. After he got his foot to one 50-50 ball and won a free kick, teammates Jérôme Rothen and Mathieu Duhamel rushed over to help him up.

'Keep it going,' Jérôme said, giving N'Golo a high-five. 'You're dragging us back into this game.'

N'Golo had a few more tricks up his sleeve, too. When Mathieu won a header in the centre-circle, N'Golo was the first to react and reach the loose ball. He dribbled further and further forward, until the Laval defenders started to close in on the edge of the penalty area.

It was time to shoot. N'Golo just had to take his time and pick his spot. BANG! The ball flew like an arrow, past the keeper's outstretched left hand, and into the bottom corner.

Goooooooooooooooooooooaaaaaaaaaaaaaaaaaallllllllllllllll llllllllllllllll!!!!!!!!!!!!!!!!!!!!!

'Get the ball,' N'Golo called out, already thinking about the next goal. Jérôme picked it out of the net as the rest of the team ran over to celebrate with him.

There was still work to do, though. N'Golo could see that the goal had dented the confidence of the Laval players – this was Caen's time to build on that goal, but time and again, they missed good chances.

'We'll get the next one!' N'Golo called out, even surprising himself. Was the underdog becoming a team leader? 'We just need one more chance.'

With just three minutes to go, Livio Nabab skipped past two tackles and whipped in a low cross. As N'Golo watched from the halfway line, Mathieu threw himself at the ball and bundled it into the net.

'Yes! Yes!' N'Golo shouted, punching the air. 'Get in!'

It was the kind of result that could change a whole season, and N'Golo felt like they had earned more than just three points as they celebrated in the dressing room.

'I couldn't be prouder right now,' Franck said as he walked into the middle of the loud room. 'Great teams fight to the very end, and that's exactly what you guys did today.'

As the wins kept coming in subsequent games, Caen were now the talk of French football, and N'Golo started to pay more attention to the league table and the newspaper articles.

'They're saying that it's just a fluky start,' he told his sister one night. 'But that's fine – I love proving people wrong!'

'I guess I'll just have to cheer even louder for you next weekend,' she replied, pausing. 'I can do that.'

'Wait, what are you talking about? I've never heard you screaming at the TV in your whole life!'

'Well I won't be watching it on TV!'

N'Golo was completely confused now. 'Wh… How…?'

'I'm going to be at the stadium, silly,' she interrupted. 'I'm visiting a friend nearby and I thought I'd come and see my big bro in action.'

N'Golo beamed. 'That's amazing! I've got to show you around. There's a market you'll love, and a nice café around the corner. Oh, and the main park is really cool.'

'OK, slow down,' his sister replied, laughing. 'I'm only there for two days! I'd settle for a nice meal and a chance to catch up.'

'Deal!' he said. 'Can't wait to see you!'

With his sister watching in the crowd, N'Golo didn't disappoint and neither did his teammates. By April, promotion was no longer a crazy idea. Caen had a real chance.

'We can't blow this now,' N'Golo told Livio as they passed the ball back and forth in training.

'Playing in Ligue 1 would be...' Livio hesitated, searching for the right word.

'... a dream come true,' Franck finished the sentence for him. 'Come on, one game at a time, boys. Don't look too far ahead.'

But that dream grew closer and closer until finally, it became a reality. Yes, Caen had successfully sealed their promotion to Ligue 1!

What an amazing achievement! There were hugs, tears, more hugs and finally a huge party – so huge that even N'Golo couldn't miss it. And he deserved it as much as anyone, if not more. He had been the core of the Caen midfield all season, starting every single match.

'We're going up! We're going up!' the players sang together as their triumph sunk in. Next season, they would be facing the best players in French football, and N'Golo couldn't wait to tackle his next big challenge.

CHAPTER 13

LEAVING FOR LEICESTER

N'Golo was in a groove now and eager to test himself against the best players in Ligue 1. He trained harder than ever during the offseason to make sure he was in top shape for the preseason schedule. As he flew around the pitch during the first session, the coaches shook their heads and laughed.

'Save something for the season!' one called out. 'We can't afford any injuries!'

'Sorry, boss,' N'Golo replied, raising his hand in apology. 'I only know one way to play.'

Ligue 1 was a big step up for the Caen players, but Franck felt sure that they could handle it: 'Show the right level of respect to these other teams, but not too much. Remember, you belong here. Stick together and we'll be just fine!'

Their 2014/15 season started with what looked like a tricky away trip to Evian. N'Golo, however, made it look as easy as a Ligue 2 game. Did he ever run out of energy? The answer was no, as he raced from box to box all game long, doing his defensive work and getting forward to help in attack.

In the twelfth minute, Caen's left winger Lenny Nangis dribbled down the line and crossed the ball to the edge of the Evian six-yard box. He was aiming for the team's star striker, Mathieu Duhamel, but instead he found... N'Golo!

But before anyone could ask why Caen's little midfielder was the furthest man forward, he swivelled his body beautifully and hit a sweet, side-foot, first-time finish into the bottom corner of the net. The goalkeeper didn't even have time to move. 1–0!

Goooooooooooooooooooooaaaaaaaaaaaaaaaaaallllllllllllll llllllllllll!!!!!!!!!!!!!!!!!!!

'Yes!' N'Golo punched the air and allowed himself a great big grin. He was very proud of his clever strike.

Then he started jogging back towards the halfway line – celebration over. But not according to his happy teammates.

'Come here, you hero!' cheered Florian Raspentino, giving him a huge hug.

'Where did that come from, hotshot?' asked Mathieu as he lifted N'Golo high into the air.

The match finished 3–0 to Caen – what a start to the season for the team, and especially for their mini midfield marvel! N'Golo was delighted with his Ligue 1 debut; it was a night that he would never, ever forget.

Too small? Too weak? No way! It felt good to be proving people wrong again, even if N'Golo did have to make a few adjustments to his game. He quickly saw that Ligue 1 players didn't fall for some of his usual tricks – like giving a few extra yards to the midfielder he was marking to tempt a defender into playing the pass, then jumping in front to intercept it.

Franck had wondered if N'Golo would have a harder time against more technical players who were bigger and stronger, but he watched in amazement as

N'Golo won the midfield battles again and again. He just always seemed to be in the right place at the right time.

In the end, Caen survived without too many scares, finishing comfortably in thirteenth place in their first season back in Ligue 1. But N'Golo had already started thinking about how the team could improve for next season when suddenly his agent, Rachid Saadna, called with some surprising news.

'N'Golo, I've had some calls with the Caen directors this morning. A few Premier League clubs have been watching you and at least one has made an offer.'

N'Golo was silent for what felt like five minutes but was probably only a few seconds. He loved watching English football, but he had never really thought about leaving France. 'Do you think Caen will accept the offer?' he eventually said in a quiet voice.

'It's hard to tell. They know that their chances of staying in Ligue 1 next year will be a lot lower if they sell you. But they also have to balance their budget and make the right decisions for the future of the club. My best guess is that the vote is narrowly split among the directors.'

N'Golo paced around the room, looking for distractions to take his mind off all the questions spinning around his head. He turned on some music but that just made him tenser. He turned on the TV in search of a football game to watch, but only found tennis. He closed his eyes and slumped back on the sofa.

Meanwhile, almost 300 miles away, Steve Walsh, Leicester City's head of recruitment, was scurrying around trying to set up a conference call with the club's top decision-makers. He had been watching N'Golo for years after first seeing him back in his Boulogne days – and he had become his biggest fan.

'The time to strike is now,' Walsh explained. There was sudden urgency, now that other clubs were circling. 'Kanté is the real deal. He does all the little things that set teams up to win. It's like there are two of him on the pitch. We could jump up the table if we put him in the centre of our midfield.'

'But he's only played one season in the top league in France,' one uncertain voice replied. 'Aren't there more experienced options available for a similar price?'

'I think it's a gamble worth taking,' another voice chimed in. 'Even if he's only half as good as you think, the price is reasonable.'

After an hour of discussion, they reached a decision. Walsh ended the call and tapped in a new phone number.

That night, N'Golo's phone buzzed. After waiting anxiously for an update all evening, and calling his agent four times just in case there was some news, he had fallen asleep. He fumbled for his phone.

'Hi, Rachid. What's up?'

Rachid laughed. 'Silly me. There I was thinking you must be doing laps of the living room waiting for my call. But you sound like you've just woken up.'

N'Golo cleared his throat to hide his embarrassment. 'Erm, I'm just doing my best to stay calm.'

'Well, you'll be pleased to hear that I have some proper news at last. Caen have accepted an offer from Leicester City. Pack your bags, you're going to be playing in the Premier League!'

N'Golo's heart skipped a beat. His first reaction was excitement, but the idea of moving again – and to a new country – was a little daunting. 'Oh wow. Is this real? Are you sure?'

'Yes, sir. It's a done deal.

'Wait, didn't they get relegated though? They were bottom of the table last time I looked.'

Rachid laughed. 'For once, I'm more up to date than you! They had a miracle escape at the end of the season and stayed up.'

'Just testing you,' N'Golo teased. 'I can't believe I'm going to be playing at Old Trafford and Anfield next season! I thought those were stadiums I'd only ever see on TV. It's going to be a special year. I can already feel it.'

With the news sinking in, N'Golo suddenly had another thought. 'Oh wait, I've got to call my family before they see the news somewhere else. I'm seeing them tomorrow, but I'll never hear the end of it if they find out about it online. If you're around tomorrow, join us to celebrate.'

'Thanks, but I've got a lot of paperwork to get

through to make sure we don't miss anything, so you'll have to start the party without me. Congrats again, N'Golo. My gut says that this is the move that will really put you on the map!'

CHAPTER 14

THE UNBELIEVABLES PART ONE

Leicester's manager Claudio Ranieri strolled into the dressing room at the end of his first training session with a big smile on his face, even though his team were the new favourites for relegation. People seemed to be so sure that they wouldn't do well that the odds of them winning the Premier League title were a whopping 5000 to 1!

But why not? Anything was possible. N'Golo was still new to the club, but he liked Claudio's positive attitude instantly.

'We all know what the story is supposed to be,' he explained slowly. 'The big teams get the top six spots and the rest of us fight for the scraps. That's fine with me. I like being the underdog. This way, they'll never see us coming!'

Claudio made a face that N'Golo guessed was meant to be like a sneaky fox. The room filled with laughter.

'Seriously, though. We have all the right ingredients to shock people this year – we can defend, we have pace, we have goalscorers. Let's go and show the world what we can do!'

The players cheered loudly, and Jamie Vardy reached over to high-five N'Golo and Riyad Mahrez. 'He's right,' Jamie said. 'We've got a really talented squad. If we get off to a good start, anything is possible!'

N'Golo started the season on the bench, but he didn't mind. He understood that he would have to earn his place in the starting line-up. Little did he know, Ranieri had already decided that N'Golo was going to be the hub of his midfield. He was the smallest player on the pitch in training, but it was immediately obvious that he was gifted in the way that he read the game.

'He just crushes the opposition's spirit with the way he breaks up every attack,' Ranieri explained to one of the coaches who had barely seen N'Golo play. 'One minute he's closing down a full back on the right, then seconds later he's clearing the ball on the left wing. It's incredible!'

By the fourth game, away to Bournemouth, N'Golo was in the starting line-up. The music was pumping, the fans were cheering – and that was just the warm-up. As N'Golo fiddled with his shin pads, he looked up at the clock in the dressing room to check how many more minutes he had to wait…

N'Golo's full Premier League debut almost ended in a loss, but thankfully, Jamie saved the day with a late penalty. 1–1 – it wasn't the win that Leicester were looking for, but N'Golo had seen enough to know that he loved the way that the team played. Now, he just needed to prove himself on the pitch and become a Leicester City legend.

A 5–2 defeat to Arsenal in September was a day to forget, but overall, N'Golo was feeling positive about life in the Premier League. Game after game, he was growing used to the speed and the style of English football. He was making more and more tackles and interceptions, and together with his partner Danny Drinkwater, he was winning more and more of his midfield battles. All that was missing now was a first Leicester goal…

At home against Watford, The Foxes were struggling to find a way through. It was still 0–0 with fifty minutes played, when the ball bounced out to N'Golo on the edge of the box.

'Shoot!' urged the Leicester supporters in the stadium.

'No, stay calm,' N'Golo told himself. He took one touch to control the ball, then another two to keep it away from the oncoming defenders. Finally, he had found a little bit of space in the crowded penalty area.

'Right, now I'll shoot!' N'Golo decided.

It wasn't the most powerful strike, or the most dangerous. In fact, the ball was trickling straight towards the Watford goalkeeper, but somehow, Heurelho Gomes let it slip through his fingers… and then through his legs. 1–0!

Goooooooooooooooooooooaaaaaaaaaaaaaaaalllllllllllll llllllllllllllll!!!!!!!!!!!!!!!!!!!!!

It wasn't the vicious, long-range volley that N'Golo had been hoping for, but still, he had scored his first Premier League goal, and he had given Leicester the lead.

'Well done, little man!' his teammates told him, throwing their arms around him. They were all delighted for their mini midfield dynamo. N'Golo was officially a club hero now.

The match ended 2–1 to Leicester, lifting them up to third place in the table. The next week, they went top after a 3–0 win at Newcastle. Wow – could they really win the league, after all? It seemed unbelievable, but their players never stopped believing.

Leicester City 1–1 Manchester United

Swansea City 0–3 Leicester City

Leicester City 2–1 Chelsea

Everton 2–3 Leicester City

The longer their strong start continued, the more

people started taking notice. Given the history of the Premier League, it was presumed that, after a while, Leicester would eventually run out of steam and slip back down the table. But N'Golo and his teammates were determined to prove people wrong. Together, they were 'The Unbelievables'.

CHAPTER 15

THE UNBELIEVABLES PART TWO

As February began, The Foxes were still there at the top of the Premier League table. It was incredible, but people were starting to really believe in 'The Unbelievables'.

'I've got a feeling they're going to win it!'

'Leicester City as the new Champions? I suppose stranger things have happened!'

By now, Manchester City were Leicester's main title rivals and Manuel Pellegrini's men, along with Tottenham and Arsenal, remained within touching distance of the top.

'This is the one,' N'Golo said to Riyad as they got onto the team bus for Leicester's showdown with

Man City at the Etihad Stadium. 'If we win today, there will be no stopping us. We'll have proven to ourselves, beyond the tiniest doubt, that we can win the title.'

'I love the way Claudio approaches these games, too – trying to win rather than just playing not to lose,' replied Riyad, who had been on an incredible run of form. 'We can really hurt them on the counter-attack with our pace. You just have to stop Agüero, David Silva and Yaya Touré. That's all!'

They both laughed. It was like taking on a fantasy football team. But as much as they respected the powerhouse clubs, there was a firm belief throughout the Leicester team that they could compete.

As the teams walked out at the Etihad, N'Golo stared straight ahead, not even looking across at the players next to him. His usual grin was nowhere to be seen. He was all business as he remembered Claudio's final words to him. 'This is your moment. Go out and set the tone. Everyone else will follow.'

They made the dream start. From a free kick on the right, Robert Huth got in front of his marker and bundled the ball into the net. 1–0!

Now Leicester had to keep their focus. N'Golo knew just charging around in midfield would not be enough. Man City were too good and too sharp. He had to be cleverer than that. His first job was to settle everyone down by keeping possession. He dropped deep to collect passes from Kasper Schmeichel and the back four, then linked up with Danny and Riyad as Leicester knocked the ball from side to side.

When City had the ball, N'Golo stuck tight to Silva, while keeping half an eye on Agüero dropping deep. Twice he was about to dart to his right and cut out dangerous through-balls. The Leicester game plan was simple when City had the ball for long spells – deny them space near the edge of the box and push forward in numbers when they won the ball back.

As N'Golo tracked another midfield run early in the second half, he saw that the ball had been under hit, allowing Wes Morgan to step forward and intercept it. N'Golo spun quickly and got into space on the left wing to receive a pass, waving his arms to get Wes's attention.

As the ball came to him, he took a confident touch forward and saw space to move into. Riyad made a run from the right and N'Golo slipped the ball through to his friend. Riyad escaped one tackle then fired an unstoppable shot into the net. 2–0!

The City fans fell silent as N'Golo joined in the celebrations near the corner flag. 'You little beauty!' he yelled, jumping on Riyad's back. 'Let's finish this. Don't let them back into the game.'

On the touchline, Claudio smiled. It was a classic Leicester goal, and now they were in control. 'City are going to have to push forward if it stays at 2–0,' he said to Craig. 'That will only open up more space for our counter-attacks.'

He was right. Every time City gave the ball away, N'Golo felt like Leicester could score. As he dropped back to allow Wes and Robert to go up for another corner, he saw Mark's corner float across. Robert was the only one to react and he guided a perfect header into the top corner. 3–0!

Unbelievable from 'The Unbelievables'! Now, Leicester could really let loose. 'Are you trying to take my spot up front?' Jamie joked, hugging Robert. The Leicester fans were going wild behind the goal, and N'Golo waved his arms to get them to cheer even louder.

Even when City pulled one goal back, Leicester didn't panic. When the final whistle sounded, N'Golo and his teammates soaked up the moment. Nobody wanted to leave the pitch after a performance like that.

'No-one can say we're not title contenders now!' N'Golo said to Jamie and Riyad. 'We're still top of the table and we're hungry for more.'

But once they had all settled down a bit in the dressing room, there was still a long way to go, as Claudio emphasised.

'I can't remember many better afternoons as a manager,' he told the team. 'But we've still got unfinished business. These signature wins are special, and you have every right to be buzzing right now – just remember that we've got thirteen more games to go. We haven't done anything yet.'

A week later, there was a very different mood in

the dressing room after Leicester threw away a 1–0 lead and lost 2–1 against Arsenal. Suddenly, the title race was wide open again – and that was all anyone wanted to talk about. N'Golo kept his phone and TV off to get away from all the stories.

'We're still in great shape,' Claudio said calmly at the next team meeting. 'We knew there would be some bumps along the way. Now we have to respond.'

As N'Golo looked around the room, he saw no fear on his teammates' faces. For all the talk about Leicester's lack of experience chasing the biggest prizes, there was a steely confidence. When his brothers asked how he was sleeping with so much at stake, N'Golo brushed off their concerns.

'Everything is going to be fine. You'll see!'

A string of 1–0 victories was exactly the reaction that Claudio wanted to see in Leicester, and Jamie always seemed to pop up with a winning goal. 'You're making our life a lot easier at the back,' Wes told N'Golo as they warmed up. 'Teams have to work so hard to get past you!'

As hard as N'Golo tried not to look at the league table, it was almost impossible as they entered the last month of the season – and he had fans reminding him everywhere he went. The different scenarios were discussed over and over again.

With Tottenham facing Chelsea on the Monday night, N'Golo accepted Jamie's invitation to watch the match together at his house with the rest of the squad. If Tottenham failed to win, Leicester would be crowned the new Premier League Champions with two games to spare. They all crowded around the TV, hoping that Chelsea would do them a favour.

The lounge went quiet as Tottenham went 2–0 up. 'Oh well, off you go, everyone,' Jamie joked, pretending to guide people towards the front door. But Chelsea were still fighting – and they pulled one goal back to create a dramatic finish.

'Come on, Chelsea!' N'Golo called out.

With just seven minutes to go, the ball found its way to Eden Hazard and, before all the players at Jamie's house really knew what was happening, the net bulged.

'Yes!' they all screamed. Others came running in to see the replay. 'We're seven minutes away from the title!'

N'Golo flashed a huge grin, then went back to anxiously watching the seconds tick down on the scoreboard.

'Come on, ref,' he shouted as he waited and waited. Finally, the final whistle sounded, confirming Leicester as Premier League champions. 'We did it! We really did it!' Kasper called out.

After a few minutes on their phones, reacting to the news with friends and family, the players joined together for some group photos.

'I still can't believe it!' Danny told N'Golo as they hugged. 'Great season, buddy. You were incredible all year.' A tray of drinks and snacks appeared as the party rumbled on.

It was only at the very end of the evening that another thought popped into N'Golo's head. 'We're going to be playing in the Champions League next season!' he called out as they all cheered again.

As he walked the short distance from his taxi

to his front door, N'Golo stopped for a moment to look up at the spectacular night sky. Stars twinkled everywhere.

'Premier League Champions,' he said to himself with a smile. 'It doesn't get much better than this.'

CHAPTER 16

LIVING IT UP WITH LES BLEUS

N'Golo had been so focused on the Premier League title race that Euro 2016 snuck up on him in a hurry. When his phone buzzed late in the season, he was finishing at the gym and almost missed the call. 'Hello?' he said, out of breath and just in time.

'Hi, N'Golo, it's Didier,' the voice on the other end said.

Didier Deschamps, the France manager! N'Golo tried not to show his surprise. 'Hi, sorry, I had to sprint for the phone.'

Didier laughed. 'I always pictured that you do everything with the same energy you show on the pitch! I won't keep you for long – I just wanted to officially confirm that you're in the France squad for Euro 2016.'

N'Golo felt a huge smile spread across his face.

'We loved how easily you slotted into the team this year and I can't wait to work with you more this summer,' Didier continued. 'I'll be announcing the squad at a press conference later today, so just keep it to yourself until then.'

His international career had been a whirlwind adventure so far. He still vividly remembered the call from Didier at the start of 2016 for his first call-up to the French squad for friendlies against the Netherlands and Russia. N'Golo had danced around the kitchen that morning, before some doubts set in over whether he would be good enough against the best players in the world.

But it was an unnecessary worry. N'Golo barely put a foot wrong in training, even after being a little star-struck for the first few hours. It was an amazing feeling to make his debut as a substitute against the Netherlands – and even more amazing to be replacing Lassana Diarra, one of his biggest childhood heroes.

'Good luck, young gun,' Lassana had told him as they high-fived on the touchline. 'This will be the first of many games you play for France.'

N'Golo still got goosebumps when he thought back to that moment.

Now, it was all about the next step: winning Euro 2016 on home soil. When he called Mama that night, she had already heard all the news.

'This is such an incredible opportunity!' she said with a mix of pride and excitement. 'This is all anyone is going to want to talk about over the next few weeks.'

N'Golo's excitement levels went up another notch when Didier announced the starting line-up for their opening game against Romania in the Stade de France. N'Golo would be in central midfield next to Paul Pogba. Didier had been very clear that he wanted this to be a new era for French football, but N'Golo had not dared to assume anything about his place in the side.

The night before the game, he put on his

headphones and lay on the bed. There was nothing more he could do to prepare – the video sessions and team meetings had covered every small detail – so he tried to think about other things. Two of his brothers would be at the game tomorrow and the rest of the family were meeting to watch together at home.

N'Golo woke early and went through his usual game day routine. He felt good in the warm-up, knocking the ball back and forth with Paul. As the anthems blared and the whole of France waited nervously, N'Golo looked around the stadium and saw blue everywhere except for a small group of Romanian fans in one corner. Even ten minutes before kick-off, it was already loud.

With N'Golo snapping into tackles and Dimitri Payet pulling the strings, France created chance after chance. Somehow, it was 1–1 as they entered the final few minutes. Sensing that the Romanian midfielders were tired, N'Golo pushed forward to support the attack, hovering around the edge of the box in case he needed to sprint back. He got to a loose pass, turned and took a quick look to see who was making an attacking run.

Olivier was being tightly marked in the box, but Dimitri was free. N'Golo rolled a simple ball to him and watched in amazement as Dimitri fired an unstoppable shot into the top corner. *2–1 to France!*

The stadium erupted in a mixture of delight and relief. 'What a goal!' N'Golo yelled, hugging Dimitri.

Back in the dressing room, Didier called for quiet. 'I loved the energy and the fight. We're going to need that every game if we want to lift the trophy. But we've got to be more ruthless when we create chances. Today, it could easily have been 5–1 with sharper finishing.'

But it was a similar story against Albania in the second group game. France controlled possession, N'Golo fed the attacking midfielders again and again, and they had twenty-one shots. Still, they needed late goals from Antoine Griezmann and Dimitri to snatch a 2–0 win.

'We're playing well all the way until we get to the edge of the box,' N'Golo told his brother that night. 'But against the best teams, we're only going to get a few chances. We can't waste them like we're doing at the moment.'

Didier rested N'Golo for the final group game, with qualification already in the bag. France went through as group winners but there were tough tests ahead. They made things much tougher by going 1–0 down to the Republic of Ireland inside the first two minutes of their Round of 16 match, after Paul gave away a penalty.

'Hey, heads up – let's go!' N'Golo called out to his teammates.

With their opponents in all-out defensive mode, Didier replaced N'Golo at half-time to add another attacking option. He watched from the bench, willing his teammates to fight back and celebrating wildly as Antoine scored twice to send France through.

Allez Les Bleus! Allez Les Bleus!

Now they were through to the quarter-finals

against Iceland. It was hard not to think (even just for a few seconds) about what it would be like to play in the final and win the tournament in front of so many home fans. N'Golo could still remember watching the World Cup Final back in 1998 with his family – what a night!

But he had forgotten one important detail: he was suspended for the next game after picking up yellow cards in the group stage and against Ireland.

As N'Golo watched his teammates cut through the Iceland defence again and again, he clapped and cheered. But on some small level, he also knew that this was going to make it very difficult for Didier to change the starting line-up for the next game, even with N'Golo available again.

Sure enough, Didier named the same team for the semi-final match against Germany – a 2–0 win, in which N'Golo came on to steady the midfield in the second half. And he picked the same team yet again for the final, a painful 1–0 loss to Portugal in extra-time that N'Golo suffered through from the subs bench.

'If only...' he kept thinking to himself.

The disappointment stung, but N'Golo still never let it affect the way he supported his teammates.

'Your teammates are lucky to have you,' Didier said to N'Golo after seeing how understanding he was about not starting in the final. 'I know this is hard but you're handling it like a real pro.'

Still, N'Golo couldn't help but wonder how the final might have been different if he had been playing.

Of course, his family had a different opinion about the whole situation.

'I'll never understand it,' one of his brothers said as they all sat down for a family meal. 'You have to play your best team in a final.'

'I think you're a bit biased!' N'Golo interrupted, before his brother could launch into another long explanation about why France would have won the final if N'Golo had played.

'Well, if we're going to go one better and win the World Cup in two years' time, they know what they need to do,' his brother said, determined to have the final word. 'They need to get N'Golo back on the pitch!'

CHAPTER 17

CHELSEA COME CALLING

As Leicester prepared for the 2016/17 season, there was one big question looming over the club like a dark cloud: would N'Golo be back for another season?

Their star midfielder was now worth five or six times more than the bargain £5.6 million that Leicester had paid for him the previous summer, and they were getting almost daily calls from teams weighing up a transfer offer. Chelsea soon shot to the top of the list and eventually clinched the deal for £32 million.

N'Golo would always love Leicester – the city, the fans, the coaches. He had so much to be thankful for. But although the club could now offer him Champions League football, N'Golo knew it was time to move on to the type of challenge that awaited at Stamford Bridge.

Chelsea were building a new team to win the title under new boss Antonio Conte. N'Golo was a key piece of that puzzle, along with the wizardry of Eden Hazard and the experience of César Azpilicueta, and he clicked with his new teammates right from the start.

'Come and see this!' Eden called out to César on the first morning of preseason. There was excitement in his voice.

César rushed over, wondering why Eden had such a big grin on his face.

'I thought he was joking about his car, but it's true!' Eden added, putting his hands on his head.

César shielded his eyes from the sun and looked across the car park. Now he understood.

On the far side, N'Golo was carefully parking what looked like a miniature version of the big, flashy cars scattered everywhere. As he opened the door, he spotted his audience and waved.

'Isn't it a beauty?' he called as he got closer to his new teammates. 'I know you love your sports cars, Eden, but that's not me. My car is small and mighty, like me!'

N'Golo flexed his muscles as Eden and César giggled.

'You're right,' Eden agreed. 'But you're probably the only footballer I know who could get away with it.'

'Is there even room for your kit in there?' César asked.

N'Golo rolled his eyes. 'Don't you start too!'

He had met most of his new Chelsea teammates at a few events during the summer, but this was his first training session with the full squad. He felt the butterflies in his stomach. No matter how many trophies he won, he hoped those kinds of nerves would always be there – it made him feel normal.

'I can't wait to get started,' N'Golo said as César guided him towards the changing rooms. 'But I'll probably get lost a few times this week. This is a really big building!'

He tried to memorise the different sections of the main building, with photos of various Chelsea legends all over the walls, but César was walking fast.

'Here we go,' César said finally, pointing to his left.

These were always the awkward moments for N'Golo. He could handle playing against the best players in the world in the noisiest stadiums in the world, but walking into a room full of people that he barely knew was scary. He took a deep breath to settle himself down, then followed César through the door.

It turned out to be easier than he had expected. After a few handshakes and some quick conversations, he found his locker and was able to start laying out his stuff. The training kit, with Number 7 on the shirt and shorts, was already folded on a shelf. The Chelsea staff were clearly doing their best to make him feel welcome.

Looking around the room, it was a bit surreal for N'Golo to see all these players that he had faced while at Leicester. Now he was one of them. Still, there were some French speakers in the squad, and he quickly got chatting with Eden and Thibaut.

When Willian spotted them, he called out: 'Uh oh, we've got a new member of the French club over here.'

Eden laughed. 'Actually, N'Golo was just saying how bad your fashion sense is. He wondered if you'd got dressed in the dark this morning!'

N'Golo fidgeted nervously and quickly wagged his finger to make it clear that Eden was making it up.

As the squad gathered in one of the big meeting rooms, Antonio marched into the room like he was late for an appointment and immediately launched into a long speech about what he hoped Chelsea would achieve during the season. He was exactly what N'Golo had expected – full of energy, full of passion and determined to fight for the Premier League title, even if they weren't the favourites.

'Lads, this is going to be a memorable year for us,' said the manager. 'I can feel it. But it all starts with what you put in during preseason. I want this group to feel like one big family. Like most families, we won't agree on everything, but we'll be just fine as long as we're honest with each other.'

The players sat quietly and listened carefully. No-one wanted to make the mistake of asking a silly question in front of the new boss. After the difficult end to the José Mourinho era, a fresh voice was always likely to give Chelsea a jolt. N'Golo hoped it would push the club all the way into the title race.

'He's a winner,' César said as the players walked to lunch. 'I think we're all going to enjoy working with him – just make sure you stay in his good books. I wouldn't want to see him angry!'

N'Golo just smiled. He liked to keep his thoughts to himself on these kinds of things, especially when he was still getting to know everyone. 'You just let your football do the talking,' as his brother liked to say.

The first training session flew by, with N'Golo determined to make a good first impression. He paired up with Eden for the passing and heading drills, watching in amazement at how easy his teammate made everything look.

'It's like the ball is glued to your foot,' he said, after one of Eden's feathery touches.

'It's funny,' Eden replied. 'To me, this is easy. It's the work you do – intercepting, tackling, racing around midfield – that feels like the hardest job.'

'Someone has to do it,' N'Golo replied with a grin. 'Then I give the ball to you and you get all the glory – not fair!'

'Sounds fair to me!' Eden said, laughing as he flicked the ball up and cushioned it softly on the back of his neck.

N'Golo had always found that playing with great players gave him more confidence to try a few tricks. As they formed a big circle and passed the ball around to avoid the two 'chasers' in the middle, he casually curled the ball to Willian with the outside of his foot and scooped another pass over the chasers' heads to César.

'Looks like you've got a few tricks up your sleeve too,' Eden called out, giving him a thumbs-up.

But it was the little five-a-side games where

N'Golo really shone.

'It's like he can see the game happening a few seconds before everyone else,' Antonio said quietly to one of his assistants. 'He was already running to intercept that pass before it left César's foot. With N'Golo protecting the defence, we should keep a lot more clean sheets.'

As he said that, N'Golo won the ball again, scampered forward and set up an easy tap-in.

'There's the reason that Leicester were so hard to beat last season,' Antonio added. 'He just pops up everywhere to win the ball back.'

CHAPTER 18

PREMIER LEAGUE CHAMPIONS AGAIN!

Antonio demanded a lot of dedication from the Chelsea players, but he did so in a way that made each of them want to run through a wall for him. N'Golo knew straight away that he had found a manager who was going to fit with his own style of play. The game plans were prepared down to the tiniest details and Antonio's motivational speeches were legendary.

But N'Golo also saw early on that it was not a good idea to get on the wrong side of his manager. Trailing 3–0 at half-time against Arsenal in late September, Antonio stormed into the dressing room.

'That was completely unacceptable!' he screamed. 'They've been quicker than us, they're working harder than us and they're laughing at us. If you guys are serious about winning the league, a half like that cannot ever happen again!'

Antonio had made his point. Now it was up to the players.

'We owe the boss and the fans better performances,' he said to Eden as they sat in the team cafeteria. 'Luckily, it's still September. There's time to turn things around.'

That week, Antonio continued his tactical changes. 'We're going to stick with the 3-4-3 formation that worked better in the second half against Arsenal. That should give us more stability at the back and help us create more down the wings.'

He looked at N'Golo. 'The downside is that you'll probably have to do even more running in midfield.'

N'Golo smiled and shrugged. 'I'm fine with that.'

Within a few weeks, N'Golo started to see the same level of confidence in the Chelsea squad that had run through the Leicester team the prior year. The new formation was helping with that, and so was the form of their mini midfield dynamo.

N'Golo won the man-of-the-match award in the 3–0 win against his old club, Leicester, and then a week later, he grabbed his first goal for the club in a 4–0 thrashing of Manchester United. Bursting onto Pedro's clever flick, N'Golo dribbled into the penalty area, past Chris Smalling, and then slid a shot past David de Gea.

Goooooooooooooooooooooaaaaaaaaaaaaaaaaaallllllllllllllllll llllllllllll!!!!!!!!!!!!!!!!!!!!

'Mate, those skills were nearly as silky as mine!' Eden congratulated him.

Soon, Chelsea climbed all the way to the top of the table, and a 2–1 win over Tottenham made it seven league wins in a row.

'We're flying now!' N'Golo said to César as they walked off the pitch together.

N'Golo had circled the next game a while ago: away to Manchester City. This would be the big test of whether Chelsea could make a title run. The early signs were troubling. They struggled to win the ball back as City pinged it from side to side, and conceded just before half-time when Gary Cahill turned the ball into his own net.

But Antonio was upbeat. 'We're riding our luck, but hang in there. Our chances will come.'

When City missed a great chance to go 2–0 up, N'Golo sensed the game might be turning. He won a couple of crunching tackles in midfield and got the ball to Cesc Fàbregas, who clipped the perfect ball towards Diego Costa. One powerful turn later, Diego smashed in the equaliser. 1–1!

'Let's go,' N'Golo yelled as he jumped on Cesc's back. 'What a pass! We've got the pace to burn them so look for that early ball every time.'

Minutes later, another counter-attack set Willian free and he fired a low shot into the bottom corner. 2–1. When Eden put the finishing touches on the comeback, N'Golo ran over to high-five Antonio. It was a classic away performance.

From there, Chelsea had all the belief they needed for the second half of the season. They stretched the winning run to thirteen straight games and let in just four goals over that span.

'Keep setting the tone in midfield,' Antonio said

after the latest intense training session. He put his arm round N'Golo. 'What would we do without you?!'

Despite a few wobbles, N'Golo and his teammates kept their nerve to seal the title. As the celebrations began, N'Golo went over to the Chelsea fans and blew kisses. For the second May in a row, he would be lifting the Premier League trophy.

There were more trophies coming too, as N'Golo was named PFA Players' Player of the Year and Football Writers' Association Footballer of the Year in recognition of the way he had guided Chelsea to the title. As he collected the awards, one journalist joked: 'So which team will you be winning the league for next season?'

N'Golo laughed. 'Chelsea, of course! I'm a true Blue now.'

CHAPTER 19

WEMBLEY WONDERLAND

Winning the 2016/17 Premier League title had been hard work, but defending the trophy proved to be even harder. Chelsea lost ten times and limped to fifth place in the table. There would be no Champions League football next season, and the pressure was mounting on Antonio.

But the FA Cup Final offered one last chance to salvage something from the season.

'Listen, things haven't gone our way this year,' Antonio said in his usual, passionate way in the Wembley dressing room just minutes before kick-off. 'But put all of that aside. It's just us against Manchester United now. One game. Ninety minutes.

Go and finish the year with a trophy.'

'Let's go!' they all shouted. N'Golo jumped up and high-fived César. 'I've got a good feeling about today,' he said. 'We're going to end the season with the FA Cup.'

César grinned. 'Didn't you say that last year, before we lost to Arsenal?'

N'Golo laughed. 'Maybe. But this time I'm not letting us lose.' He pulled his socks up and joined the rest of the team in the tunnel. Even after all the big games he had played in over the past two seasons, he still felt the butterflies in his stomach.

As usual, the nerves disappeared after the first couple of passes. He had plenty of work to do, with Alexis Sánchez and Marcus Rashford dropping short and making clever runs. As the ball flew out of play for a throw-in, N'Golo stopped as he jogged past Cesc. 'If you see Eden one-on-one against Phil Jones, send the pass early,' he said. 'He's already burned him for pace twice.'

Cesc nodded and barely two minutes later he whipped a pass behind the United defence. Eden was chasing it in a flash, with Jones wheezing behind him. Just as Eden was about to shoot, N'Golo saw Jones lunge across and trip him up. Penalty!

He looked over at Cesc and winked. Cesc gave him a thumbs-up in reply. Eden brushed the grass off his shoulder and stroked the penalty into the corner. 1–0!

At half-time, Antonio looked as happy as N'Golo could remember seeing him that whole season. 'That was a terrific half,' he said, pacing from one side of the room to the other. 'Keep the energy up and don't take any silly risks. We've got one hand on the trophy.'

N'Golo buzzed around at the start of the second half. He knew United would try to make a fast start, but he won every ball that bounced in midfield, even barging Cesc out of the way to win one header.

With the clock ticking down, he surged forward and saw that United were outnumbered. N'Golo's first instinct was always to find a quick pass but now he had to look for a shot. As he pulled his leg back to aim for the bottom corner, a United defender suddenly lunged forward. N'Golo saw it just in time and rolled the ball to his right to Marcos Alonso. Just as Marcos sensed his moment of glory, the ball was scrambled clear. 'Argh!' N'Golo shouted, wishing he had taken an earlier shot.

In the end, it didn't matter. The whistle blew and N'Golo had won the FA Cup for the first time! He climbed the famous Wembley steps and lined up for his medal – it was all just like he had pictured after seeing it on TV so many times. As the medal was placed around his neck, he grinned and turned to face the cheering Chelsea fans.

Gary lifted the FA Cup high in the air as blue and white confetti appeared out of nowhere. When N'Golo and Antonio hugged on the pitch, it was hard to know what the future held.

'Whatever happens next, it has been a real honour to play for you,' N'Golo said.

Antonio looked at his star midfielder with a sad look on his face. 'No, it's been my honour to coach you!' he said, patting N'Golo on the back and walking towards the tunnel.

CHAPTER 20

ON TOP OF THE WORLD

Hot on the heels of the FA Cup glory, N'Golo prepared for the next test: the 2018 World Cup. When the France squad arrived in Russia, the memories of falling just short at Euro 2016 were still fresh for most of the squad. 'We can't take anything for granted,' Paul Pogba explained. 'We're one of the favourites but that counts for nothing when the games start.'

N'Golo nodded wearily. Like so many of his teammates, he was arriving in Russia after a gruelling league season, but this was not the time for tired legs. After a few table tennis tournaments and FIFA battles at the team hotel, the competitive juices were flowing again.

France had been drawn in Group C along with
Denmark, Australia and Peru, and there were
never any easy games at this stage. As N'Golo sat
in his hotel room the night before their first game –
against Australia – he took a moment to soak up the
experience. He was about to play at the World Cup!

There was a knock on the door. N'Golo swung
himself off the bed and opened it. It was Kylian
Mbappé. 'Can't sleep either?' he asked his young
teammate.

Kylian shook his head. 'My mind is racing. I'm
excited, nervous, tired and alert all at once. Any
suggestions? Just don't say counting sheep.'

N'Golo laughed. 'Well there goes my best idea!
Have you tried listening to some meditation music?
That might help you relax.'

'Okay, I'll give that a try,' Kylian replied. 'So why
are you still awake?'

'Kind of the same reason as you, to be honest. I
know tomorrow is going to be a total blur so I'm
trying to enjoy the moment before the pressure

cranks up a few extra levels.'

The bus was very quiet on the way to the stadium. N'Golo looked out of the window as they crawled through traffic in the city centre. He could see a few French flags among the crowds of football fans rushing to get food and drink before the game.

When he walked into the dressing room, he froze. The third locker on the left-hand side had the KANTÉ shirt hung up ready for him. He snapped a quick photo and then started changing for the warm-up.

The noise was deafening as the players walked onto the pitch, each of them hand-in-hand with a young mascot. 'This is what it's all about,' N'Golo whispered under his breath. He knocked the ball around with Paul and Kylian, just to pass the time as they waited for kick-off.

The first half was instantly forgettable, but France came roaring out for the second half, winning a penalty when Antoine was bundled over in the box. Soon, though, N'Golo had his head in his hands as Australia levelled the score. This wasn't how their

tournament was supposed to start, and it brought
back memories of their shaky start to Euro 2016.

Once the rust from the first game had passed,
N'Golo felt more at ease. France clinched top spot
in Group C with a 1–0 win over Peru and a goalless
draw against Denmark, even as they still searched
for their best form. 'Now it's time for the big tests,'
he said to Paul as they picked up snacks back at the
hotel. 'We've been able to get away with playing
in third gear. That won't be good enough in the
knockout rounds.'

He was right. France stuttered against Argentina
in the second round, falling 2–1 behind early in the
second half. Fans around the world waited on the
edge of their seats to see how they would respond.
'Settle it down!' N'Golo called to Raphaël Varane
after one wild clearance. 'We've got lots of time.'

Didier was on the touchline, signalling for the
French full backs to push forward. He pointed at
N'Golo. 'As they push up, you drop in to cover.'

That plan started to work. N'Golo tucked in
to keep an eye on Lionel Messi, while Benjamin

Pavard and Lucas Hernandez flew forward to make overlapping runs. Twice, Benjamin turned to sprint back, but N'Golo raised his hand each time. 'Don't worry. I'm here.'

A minute later, the ball dropped to Benjamin who was still up the field supporting the attack. He fired a fierce shot that arrowed into the top corner. From that point on, N'Golo felt the confidence flow back into the team. Kylian scored twice in four minutes and suddenly it was 4–2.

'When we play like we did in the second half, no one can touch us in this tournament,' Didier said, clapping as he spoke. 'We scored three, but we could have had ten.'

'Blame Olivier,' Antoine shouted, making everyone giggle.

Olivier Giroud pretended to look upset. 'If it's not a header, don't give me the ball,' he joked. 'Don't you know that by now?'

N'Golo sat quietly, enjoying the banter between his teammates and stretching out his sore calves. He had already made sure he was at the front of the line for a post-game massage and was thankful to have almost a week before the quarter-final.

For the next few days, it was all about Uruguay. 'I've watched a lot of the clips from their games so far and we should have a real advantage in midfield,' N'Golo said to Paul as they finished another lap of the pitch. 'We're more physical and more experienced. That's where the game will be won.'

As usual, N'Golo barely put a foot wrong. He loved playing next to Paul and being able to lay the ball off to him when he won it back. Just before half-time, Antoine lined up a free kick on the right. 'Get in there,' N'Golo called to Raphaël and Samuel Umtiti, who both seemed unsure about whether to join the strikers in the box. N'Golo dropped back as the last line of defence. Antoine whipped the ball across and Raphaël got in front of his marker to head the ball in.

'I told you!' N'Golo called as he ran towards Raphaël. 'That's why we need you in the box!'

Antoine doubled the lead in the second half after

a goalkeeping blunder and N'Golo took particular pride in the clean sheet.

'We had to tighten up after the way we played against Argentina,' N'Golo told Luc, his old friend who had called to get the latest behind-the-scenes updates.

'There must be days when you have to pinch yourself to believe it was only a few years ago that you were playing for JS Suresnes!'

'Basically every day!' N'Golo replied. 'Now we're one game away from the World Cup final. That still sounds ridiculous to say out loud!'

With the pressure rising, N'Golo found himself sleeping less and less. 'We need something to get our minds off football for a few hours,' he told Paul at breakfast one morning.

'Consider it done,' Paul replied, with a mischievous grin. 'I've got lots of ideas.'

N'Golo rolled his eyes. 'Oh no, I should have kept quiet.'

That night, Paul called all the players to one of the hotel meeting rooms where he had set up a karaoke machine and four microphones. 'Sunday is going to be the biggest game of our lives, and the pressure is only going to get more intense as we get closer to kick-off,' he said, speaking into one of the microphones. 'So let's forget about all that tonight and have some fun!'

He threw the other three microphones to Antoine, Kylian and Hugo Lloris, and pressed a button to select the first song. As N'Golo joined in with the singing and dancing, it felt good to just have some laughs with his teammates.

The next day, it was back to serious work. N'Golo spent hours watching clips of Modrić from the tournament, prepared by the team's video crew. 'Look for the areas where he likes to receive the ball and ways that we can take him out of his comfort zone,' Didier suggested. As a former midfielder himself, Didier had helped N'Golo see the game even more clearly over the last few weeks.

The four days between the semi-final and final felt like two weeks for N'Golo, but Sunday finally arrived. The France bus pulled up at the stadium, where crowds of fans were already lined up to welcome them. N'Golo slipped off his headphones and signed a few autographs on the way inside. To play in a World Cup final was a dream come true – and he was determined to enjoy every moment.

After taking a quick look at the pitch and getting set up at his locker, N'Golo went out for the warm-up. It was a beautiful sunny day and the atmosphere was already building, with fans and volunteers gathered around the edge of the pitch. He thought back to two years ago and the pain of warming up for the Euro 2016 final as a substitute. This time, he had earned his place in the starting line-up.

Didier kept the pre-game team talk short. He knew his players did not need to be pumped up for a World Cup final. 'Let's play the game on our terms,' he said calmly. 'Press them in midfield, get the ball wide and let our attackers take over. I'm so proud of this whole group for what you've achieved over the past three weeks. Now let's finish the job.'

Standing in the tunnel, N'Golo stretched his neck from side to side, trying to shake out some of the nerves. This was it. This was what he had worked for year after year. One of the FIFA representatives appeared with a group of young boys and girls who would be walking out with the players. N'Golo shook hands with the little boy he was paired with. As the referee led the two lines of players forward, N'Golo took a deep breath and held hands with the little boy. The boy's big smile was contagious. N'Golo smiled back. This was a special moment for everyone.

The game got off to a breathless start, with N'Golo in the thick of the midfield action. It was a roller coaster first half as France went ahead, Croatia pulled level, then France grabbed a second goal. N'Golo was furious with himself for not doing better on Croatia's goal. He rushed out to block the shot but he was too late. Still, his number one job was to keep close to Modrić and he did that expertly.

By the time France put the finishing touches on

the win, N'Golo was resting his legs on the bench.
He jumped up when Kylian fired in the fourth goal
and talked excitedly with the subs. They were
all counting the minutes to when they would get
their hands on the World Cup trophy. When the
referee blew the final whistle, N'Golo raced onto
the pitch to celebrate with his teammates, hugging
Paul and Kylian, then Antoine and Olivier. 'We've
won the World Cup!' Olivier shouted. 'Is this really
happening?'

'It doesn't get any better than this!' N'Golo yelled
back.

When the trophy was passed to him, N'Golo took
a moment to admire the shiny gold. 'Wow!' he said
to himself. He kissed it and raised it high into the
air.

The party went on late into the night as the new
World Cup winners enjoyed every moment. But
nothing prepared N'Golo for the scenes in Paris
when they returned home with the trophy.

'This is unbelievable!' he said to Paul as they
waved to the huge crowd that had gathered on all

sides of their bus parade. 'What a feeling to know that this means so much to so many people!'

CHAPTER 21

TROPHY TIME AGAIN

As N'Golo had feared, Antonio was replaced as
Chelsea manager in that summer of 2018, with
Maurizio Sarri taking over. Though Maurizio had
coached in Italy's Serie A, like Antonio, it was a big
change for all the players. For a start, N'Golo was
asked to play a slightly different position, as more of a
box-to-box midfielder, instead of an anchorman.

'I've watched you loads of times and you're a great
passer,' Maurizio explained. 'I want to press the ball
further up the pitch and then get you in positions to
set up the strikers. Let's see how it goes.'

N'Golo nodded. He had his doubts about taking on
more creative responsibilities, but he was willing to

give it a try if it helped the team.

In the first few games, he couldn't get it quite right. 'I always feel like I'm either too far forward or too far back,' he told César at training one morning. 'It still doesn't feel natural to be in the box so much.'

'Yeah, but you're a deadly goalscorer now!' César replied, laughing. N'Golo had tucked away a volley in the first game of the season against Huddersfield and his teammates couldn't stop talking about it. They loved to act it out in training.

Even with N'Golo getting more comfortable in his new role, Chelsea were soon way off the pace in the Premier League, with Liverpool and Manchester City storming ahead at the top of the table. Before long, criticism of Maurizio's tactics got louder and louder. Like the previous season, Chelsea had to throw everything at the cup competitions.

That worked in their favour in the Europa League, as some teams rested their regular starters for the gruelling midweek trips. But N'Golo was pleased that the club was taking it seriously. After a nervy penalty shoot-out win over Eintracht Frankfurt, Chelsea reached the final where they would face local rivals Arsenal.

'I wish we'd been fighting for the Premier League title this year, but another major final isn't a bad consolation prize,' N'Golo said to Willian as they boarded the plane.

'I know,' he replied. 'We kind of take these games for granted these days. Some players have long careers and don't ever get to experience a big final like this.'

Maurizio got the players fired up as they took their last sips from their water bottles before walking out to the tunnel. 'We've had ups and downs this year, but let's end it on a high note. The fans have come a long way for this final – make sure they head home with London bragging rights!'

Then came the knock on the door from the match-day officials. It was time. N'Golo shook hands with a few familiar faces in the Arsenal team as they waited, side-by-side. Tomorrow, they would all be friends again, but for the next ninety minutes, they were the enemy. It was odd to be playing in a big European final against a team from their own league. He just hoped the Arsenal players didn't know him and his teammates too well.

After a goalless first half, Chelsea tore Arsenal apart. N'Golo had a feeling this would be Eden's last game for the club and he watched in amazement as his teammate served up yet another special performance. N'Golo just focused on winning the ball back and finding Eden. When he was playing like this, it was like he was playing a different sport from everyone else.

By the time Eden scored his second goal of the night to make it 4–1, N'Golo could already hear the Chelsea fans starting the party. It was the perfect way to seal the win as they all slid to celebrate with Eden near the corner flag. The Arsenal end of the stadium emptied in a hurry.

N'Golo could see how much the night meant to Maurizio – it was his first major trophy as a manager and he had a big smile plastered on his face. He ran over to his manager and wrapped him in a hug. 'We did it!' N'Golo shouted, taking Maurizio's arm and urging him to come over to the Chelsea fans to join in the celebrations. 'Come on, you deserve to be with us.'

As they walked over, Maurizio looked at N'Golo and smiled. 'You've won the Premier League twice, the FA Cup and the World Cup, but you still look as thrilled as me!'

'It never gets old,' he said, shrugging. 'What else can I say? I just love winning!'

They both laughed as they waved to the Chelsea fans and got ready for the trophy presentation.

CHAPTER 22

A FRESH START WITH FRANK

N'Golo had been at Chelsea long enough to know that managers tended to change on a regular basis, so it was no big surprise when Maurizio Sarri left the club after just one season. It did not take long for the next target to emerge: Chelsea legend Frank Lampard.

N'Golo had never played against him but he knew all about his special history with the club.

'I'm thrilled to be back here and to have the chance to work with you all,' Frank explained at his meeting with the squad. 'We've got a lot of work to do, but we're going to have fun along the way.'

N'Golo was eager to see how he would fit into

Frank's plans. Under Maurizio, he had been given a more advanced midfield role, with Jorginho playing as the holding midfielder. He had enjoyed the chance to get forward more, and even scored a few goals, but he still felt his best position was just in front of the defence. That was where he won the most battles for the ball.

One place he did not expect to be was on the bench – so it came as a shock when Frank picked younger midfield options for the first game of the season away to Manchester United. N'Golo had dealt with injuries during the preseason and Frank explained that he wanted to give him more time to recover. But a thumping 4–0 loss got the season off to a shaky start.

'We've got to guide the younger players through this,' N'Golo told César as they jogged round the pitch together at training the next week. 'There's a lot of talent in this squad – Tammy Abraham, Christian Pulisic, Mason Mount – but winning consistently takes time. It's normal to have some rough weeks.'

César nodded. 'In the meantime, we've got to keep picking up points to take the heat off Frank.'

Gradually, Chelsea got their season on track. Tammy was banging in the goals and, after missing a few games with an ankle issue, N'Golo was back to patrol the midfield. With Manchester United, Tottenham and Arsenal faltering, the Blues climbed into the top four. 'Things are starting to click,' he said at the next team meeting.

Like Maurizio had done, Frank frequently played N'Golo next to Jorginho, encouraging him to make forward bursts. 'It's nice to remind people sometimes that I can do more than tackle!' he told Frank when they talked through the tactics.

Away to a struggling Southampton side, N'Golo got plenty of chances to surge into the box. Just before half-time, he took a pass from Marcos and looked up. No-one was coming to close him down, so he took another touch towards the target. As defenders continued to back away, he lined up a shot and watched as it flicked off a defender and flew into the net.

Goooooooooooooooooooooaaaaaaaaaaaaaaaaallllllllllll llllllllllllllll!!!!!!!!!!!!!!!!!!!!

After the heavy deflection, he didn't feel like he should celebrate too much, but it still counted as his goal.

'This is more like it,' N'Golo said to Frank as they walked to the team bus. 'We're playing like a top four team now!'

Though Liverpool were running away with the title race, the Frank era was off to a promising start. 'Next season, we're going to take some stopping,' he told his family when they gathered in Paris for Mama's birthday. 'It's going to be a big year.'

They all smiled at N'Golo's competitive nature. Winning trophies was always on his mind.

'Are you laughing at me?!' he said, sensing what they were thinking. 'I just love helping my team to succeed. What's wrong with that?'

'Nothing, sweetie,' Mama replied, hugging him. 'Just remember that what you've already achieved is incredible. I can still picture the night when you

first told me that you wanted to be a footballer
– now look at you. You've won the World Cup,
you've won the Premier League twice, and you've
received all kinds of individual awards.'

N'Golo smiled. Sometimes he needed that
kind of reminder. 'You're right. It's been quite a
journey, and I couldn't have done any of it without
you all.'

He paused, suddenly shy about all the attention
he was getting. 'Oh, look at all these presents,' he
said, changing the subject. 'Why don't you open
some of them, Mama?'

Typical N'Golo. They all laughed at the little boy
who had battled his way to the top and become a
brilliant (but still modest) superstar.

Turn the page for a sneak preview of
another brilliant football story by
Matt and Tom Oldfield. . .

MBAPPÉ

Available now!

CHAPTER 1

FROM RUSSIA WITH LOVE

On 14 July 2018, Kylian sent a message to his millions of social media followers, from Russia with love: 'Happy French national day everyone. Let's hope the party continues until tomorrow night!'

'Tomorrow night' – 15 July – the French national team would be playing in the World Cup final at the Luzhniki Stadium in Moscow. It was the most important football match on the planet and Kylian's country was counting on him.

So far, he hadn't let them down at all. In fact, Kylian had been France's speedy superstar, scoring the winning goal against Denmark, and then two more in an amazing man-of-the-match performance against Argentina. That all made him the nation's best 'Number 10' since Zinedine Zidane back in 1998.

That was the year that France last won the World Cup.

That was also the year that Kylian was born.

Thanks to their new young superstar, '*Les Bleus*' were now the favourites to lift the famous golden trophy again. They had already beaten Lionel Messi's Argentina, Luis Suárez's Uruguay in the quarter-finals, and Eden Hazard's Belgium in the semi-finals. Now, the only nation standing in their way was Luka Modrić's Croatia.

'You've done so well to get this far,' the France manager, Didier Deschamps, told them as kick-off approached and the nerves began to jangle. 'Now, you just need to go out there and finish off the job!'

A massive 'Yeah!' echoed around the room. It was one big team effort, from captain Hugo Lloris in goal through to Kylian, Antoine Griezmann and Olivier Giroud in attack. Everyone worked hard and everyone worked together.

By the way, those jangling nerves didn't

belong to Kylian. No way, he was the coolest character around! He never let anything faze him. When he was younger, he hadn't just hoped to play in a World Cup final; he had expected it. It was all part of his killer plan to conquer the football world.

Out on the pitch for the final in Moscow, Kylian sang the words of the French national anthem with a big smile on his face. As a four-year-old, some people had laughed at his ambitious dreams. Well, they definitely weren't laughing now.

'Right, let's do this!' Paul Pogba clapped and cheered as they took up their positions. His partnership with Kylian would be key for France. Whenever Paul got the ball in midfield, he would look to find his pacy teammate with a perfect pass.

Kylian's first action of the final, however, was in defence. He rushed back quickly to block a Croatia cross.

'Well done!' France's centre-back Samuel Umtiti shouted.

Once that was done, it was all about attacking.

Even in a World Cup final, Kylian wasn't afraid to try his tricks and flicks. They didn't always work but it was worth the risk.

It was an end-to-end first half, full of exciting action. First, Antoine curled in a dangerous free kick and Mario Mandžukić headed the ball into his own net. 1–0 to France! Kylian punched the air – what a start!

Ivan Perišić equalised for Croatia but then he handballed it in his own box. Penalty! Antoine stepped up... and scored – 2–1 to France!

The players were happy to hear the half-time whistle blow. They needed a break to breathe and regroup. Although France were winning, they still had work to do if they wanted to become World Champions again.

'We need to calm things down and take control of the game,' Deschamps told his players. 'Stay smart out there!'

Kylian listened carefully to his manager's message. He needed to relax and play to his strengths – his skill but also his speed. This was his chance to go down in World Cup history:

Pelé in 1958,

Diego Maradona in 1986,

Zidane in 1998,

Ronaldo in 2002,

Kylian in 2018?

In the second half, France's superstars shone much more brightly. Kylian collected Paul's long pass and sprinted straight past the Croatia centre-back. Was he about to score in his first World Cup final? No, the keeper came out to make a good save.

'Ohhhh!' the supporters groaned in disappointment.

But a few minutes later, Paul and Kylian linked up again. From wide on the right wing, Kylian dribbled towards goal. Uh oh, the Croatia left-back was in big trouble.

With a stepover and a little hop, Kylian cut inside towards goal but in a flash, he fooled the defender with another quick change of direction.

'Go on!' the France fans urged their exciting

young hero.

What next? Kylian still had two defenders in front of him, so he pulled it back to Antoine instead. He couldn't find a way through either so he passed it on to Paul. Paul's first shot was blocked but his second flew into the bottom corner. 3–1!

Kylian threw his arms up in the air and then ran over to congratulate his friend. Surely, France had one hand on the World Cup trophy now.

Antoine had scored, and so had Paul. That meant it must be Kylian's turn next! He would have to score soon, however, in case Deschamps decided to take him off early...

When he received the pass from Lucas Hernández, Kylian was in the middle of the pitch, at least ten yards outside the penalty area. Was he too far out to shoot? No, there was no such thing as 'too far' for Kylian! He shifted the ball to the right and then BANG! He tucked the ball into the bottom corner before the keeper could even dive. 4–1!

Goooooooooooooooooooooaaaaaaaaaaaaaaaaallllllllllll llllllllllllllll!!!!!!!!!!!!!!!!!!!!

As his teammates rushed over to him, Kylian had
just enough time for his trademark celebration. With
a little jump, he planted his feet, folded his arms
across his chest, and tried to look as cool as he could.
That last part was really hard because he had just
scored in a World Cup final!

The next thirty minutes ticked by very slowly but
eventually, the game was over. France 4 Croatia 2 –
they were the 2018 World Champions!

Allez Les Bleus! Allez Les Bleus! Allez Les Bleus!

Kylian used the last of his energy to race around
the pitch, handing out hugs to everyone he saw: his
sad opponents, his happy teammates, his manager,
EVERYONE! In that amazing moment, he would
have hugged every single French person in the world
if he could. Instead, he blew kisses at the cameras.
From Russia with love!

And Kylian's incredible night wasn't over yet.
Wearing his country's flag around his waist, he
walked up on stage to collect the tournament's Best
Young Player award from Emmanuel Macron.

'Thank you, you're a national hero now!' the French President told him proudly.

'My pleasure, Sir!' Kylian replied.

Would his smile ever fade? Certainly not while he had a World Cup winners' medal around his neck and the beautiful World Cup trophy in his hands. He didn't ever want to let go. Kylian kissed it and raised it high into the Moscow night sky.

'Hurray!' the fans cheered for him.

At the age of nineteen, Kylian was already living out his wildest dreams. The boy from Bondy had become a World Cup winner and football's next great superstar.

Leicester City

🏆 Premier League: 2015–16

Chelsea

🏆 Premier League: 2016–17
🏆 FA Cup: 2017–18
🏆 UEFA Europa League: 2018–19

France

🏆 FIFA World Cup: 2018

Individual

🏆 PFA Premier League Team of the Year: 2015–16, 2016–17
🏆 Leicester City Players' Player of the Year: 2015–16

🏆 PFA Players' Player of the Year: 2016–17

🏆 Premier League Player of the Season: 2016–17

🏆 FWA Footballer of the Year: 2016–17

🏆 Chelsea Players' Player of the Year: 2016–17

🏆 French Player of the Year: 2017

🏆 Chelsea Player of the Year: 2017–18

🏆 UEFA Team of the Year: 2018

🏆 ESPN Midfielder of the Year: 2019

KANTE

4 THE FACTS

NAME: N'GOLO KANTÉ

DATE OF BIRTH: 29 March 1991

AGE: 28

PLACE OF BIRTH: Paris

NATIONALITY: French

BEST FRIEND: Riyad Mahrez

CURRENT CLUB: Chelsea

POSITION: CM

THE STATS

Height (cm):	168
Club appearances:	322
Club goals:	22
Club trophies:	4
International appearances:	39
International goals:	1
International trophies:	1
Ballon d'Ors:	0

★ ★ ★ **HERO RATING: 90** ★ ★ ★

GREATEST MOMENTS

9 AUGUST 2014, ÉVIAN THONON GAILLARD 0–3 SM CAEN

After three seasons starring in the lower divisions of French football, this was finally N'Golo's Ligue 1 debut. And after only twelve minutes, he was already celebrating his first Ligue 1 goal. As a cross came into the box, he swivelled his body beautifully and scored with a first-time, side-foot finish. Soon, Leicester City came calling...

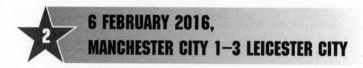

6 FEBRUARY 2016,
MANCHESTER CITY 1–3 LEICESTER CITY

This was the day when Leicester showed that they really could go on and win the Premier League title. Although N'Golo didn't score this time, he certainly played his part in the victory. He won the midfield battle against Fernandinho and Yaya Touré, and he even set up the second goal for Riyad Mahrez. Three months later, Leicester were crowned Champions.

23 OCTOBER 2016,
CHELSEA 4–0 MANCHESTER UNITED

Following an embarrassing 3–0 defeat to Arsenal, Chelsea knew that they had to turn things around. Their manager Antonio Conte changed the formation, and their mini midfield dynamo N'Golo found his top form again. This classy finish was the start of an incredible run that ended with him winning his second Premier League title in two years.

19 MAY 2018,
CHELSEA 1–0 MANCHESTER UNITED

After the disappointment of losing the 2017 FA Cup
Final to Arsenal, Chelsea bounced back to make it to
Wembley again the next year. This time, they were
determined to win, and N'Golo's tough tackling in
midfield helped lead them to a 1–0 victory.

15 JULY 2018,
FRANCE 4–2 CROATIA

Two years after watching the Euro 2016 Final from
the subs bench, N'Golo was starting for France in the
World Cup Final. What a night! He wasn't one of the
stand-out stars, but he did his defensive work brilliantly,
winning the midfield battle against Luka Modrić. And
earning himself a World Cup winner's medal.

PLAY LIKE YOUR HEROES

N'GOLO KANTÉ'S BATTLING TO WIN THE BALL

STEP 1: Start by working hard on your fitness because you're going to have lots of running to do...

STEP 2: Always stay alert and in position. Sometimes you might not have that much ball-winning to do, but when your team needs you, they'll really need you!

STEP 3: When your opponents do attack, race over to the danger but don't dive in straight away. You've got to read the situation carefully first.

STEP 4: If your opponent decides to dribble with the ball, use your speed to chase him down and then time your tackle to perfection. BALL WON BACK!

STEP 5: If your opponent decides to play a pass instead, use your football brain to guess where the ball is going and then get there first. BALL WON BACK!

STEP 6: As soon as you can, give the ball to your team's skillful attackers and watch them get all the glory.

STEP 7: There's no time for celebrations. Remember, you're an unsung hero and your work isn't done until the match is over and all the ball battles have been won.

TEST YOUR KNOWLEDGE

QUESTIONS

1. What match in 1998 inspired N'Golo to be a footballer for France?

2. What was the one position that N'Golo didn't want to play at JS Suresnes?

3. Which Le Havre player became N'Golo's midfield hero?

4. How old was N'Golo when he moved to Boulogne?

5. And how did N'Golo travel to training at first?

6. How many seasons did N'Golo spend at Caen?

7. How much did Leicester City pay to sign N'Golo in 2015?

8. How much did Chelsea pay to sign N'Golo one year later?

9. How many Premier League titles has N'Golo won so far?

10. True or false – N'Golo played for France in the Euro 2016 Final.

11. Who was N'Golo's main midfield partner for France at the 2018 World Cup?

Answers below. . . No cheating!

1. *The World Cup Final* 2. *Goalkeeper* 3. *Lassana Diarra* 4. *Nineteen years old* 5. *On a micro scooter!* 6. *Two seasons in total – one in Ligue 2 and one in Ligue 1* 7. *£5.6 million* 8. *£32 million!* 9. *Two* 10. *False – he was on the bench, but he didn't come on* 11. *Paul Pogba*